"For those of us who did our theological training in the mid-sixties, Francis Schaeffer stood as beacon of light and clarity in the midst of such nonsense as situation ethics and the death of God. His analysis of our cultural drift and deterioration, and eventual self-destruction, had the double authority of biblical truth and disciplined reason. My dog-eared copy of *The God Who Is There* has a very rusty paper clip on the page where Schaeffer says, 'The Christian is to resist the spirit of the world. But when we say this we must understand that the world-spirit does not always take the same form. So the Christian must resist the spirit of the world *in the form it takes in his own generation.*' Schaeffer gave us some of the best tools and weapons we need to do just that."
BISHOP JOHN W. HOWE, *Episcopal Diocese of Central Florida*

"Although we never met, Francis Schaeffer was my first intellectual mentor. Reading *The God Who Is There* a few months after my conversion in 1976 sparked in me a grand vision for ministry that has never dimmed. Schaeffer argued that Christianity is objectively true and rational and that it uniquely provides hope and meaning that secular culture desperately needs. Christians should outthink the world for the sake of Christ's kingdom! As a college student majoring in philosophy at a secular university, I devoured Schaeffer's many books. Although they didn't answer all my questions, they gave me a framework for keeping both my intellectual integrity and biblical orthodoxy. Thirty years after its publication, the message of *The God Who Is There* still needs to be heard and heeded."
DOUGLAS GROOTHUIS, *Associate Professor of Philosophy of Religion and Ethics, Denver Seminary*

"It is good in every sense to see a thirtieth-anniversary edition of this book. Although I continue to differ pretty seriously with Francis Schaeffer on many details in his writings— and maybe even on a few points that are not details— I also continue to think that Schaeffer's influence was entirely positive on the broader evangelical community. At a time when very few evangelical voices really engaged the world as it had come to exist, Schaeffer's steely resolve to do so in the powerful integrity of the gospel was a godsend for which all who honor Christ as the way, the truth and the life must be eternally grateful."
MARK A. NOLL, *Professor of History, Wheaton College*

"I was with Francis Schaeffer in Switzerland on and off for a number of years in the sixties while his ideas were being developed and prior to any of his books' being published. What attracted me to him was the way he could make classical Christianity more interesting and plausible than your average postfundamentalist, and the way he would interact with liberal theology and secular thought somewhat on their level.

He was my Paul Tillich, moving back and forth between questions
of the culture and answers from the Bible. He set me a good example,
not to imitate but to follow."
CLARK PINNOCK, *Professor of Theology, McMaster Divinity College,
Hamilton, Ontario*

"Francis Schaeffer's books sparked my first love of philosophy.
And now, having become a public philosopher, I have an ever deeper
appreciation for the importance of his impact on a whole generation
of educated Christians, as well as on a broader audience.
He sparked many of us to think in new ways and can continue
to do so for yet another generation of readers."
TOM MORRIS, *Chairman, Morris Institute and author of* If Aristotle Ran
General Motors

"As an evangelical student in a liberal divinity school in the late 1950s,
I was largely in a defensive mode, like many others in a similar situation.
My personal encounter with Francis Schaeffer in 1961 helped me
to gain the confidence that evangelical faith does not need to be afraid
of encountering the unbelieving world. One of Francis Schaeffer's
comments was, 'We must not be afraid to get shot at.' Since I was a near
neighbor of his from 1965 onward while working at the IFES office in
Lausanne, Switzerland, I was among many who encouraged him to get his
ideas into print, in order that not merely a few visitors to L'Abri but a whole
generation might enjoy the same encouragement. The publication of
The God Who Is There, following right after his shorter first work,
Escape from Reason, put his clear, uncompromising and supernaturally
confident thinking before a wider public. It came out thirty years ago,
but it has aged well and is no less valuable today than it was then."
HAROLD O. J. BROWN, *Professor of Biblical and Systematic Theology,
Trinity Evangelical Divinity School*

"No one has more profoundly influenced my ministry than
Francis Schaeffer, the great prophet of our age. If the one result of
my writings and ministry were to get people to read Schaeffer,
I'd consider my work fully rewarded."
CHARLES COLSON, *Prison Fellowship Ministries, Washington, D.C.*

"For many Christians in my generation, Dr. Francis Schaeffer
was the single most significant person to begin to challenge us
to think about all of life in a consistently Christian way. Along with
C. S. Lewis, Francis Schaeffer has been the most significant Christian
apologist of our time. He grappled with all the current issues from
a consistently biblical and reformational perspective and led those
who read him not only to think but also to act in a Christian manner.
We are deeply in his debt."
JAMES MONTGOMERY BOICE, *Senior Minister, Tenth Presbyterian
Church, Philadelphia*

The God Who Is There

FRANCIS A. SCHAEFFER

30TH ANNIVERSARY EDITION

InterVarsity Press
Downers Grove, Illinois

InterVarsity Press
P.O. Box 1400, Downers Grove, IL 60515
World Wide Web: www.ivpress.com
E-mail: mail@ivpress.com

Introduction: ©1998 by InterVarsity Christian Fellowship/USA
First Edition: ©1968 by L'Abri Fellowship.
Second Edition: ©1982 by Francis A. Schaeffer. Revised text graciously provided by Crossway Books, Wheaton, Illinois.

Printed in America by InterVarsity Press®, Downers Grove, Illinois, with permission from Hodder and Stoughton, Limited, England.

InterVarsity Press® is the book-publishing division of InterVarsity Christian Fellowship/USA®, a student movement active on campus at hundreds of universities, colleges and schools of nursing in the United States of America, and a member movement of the International Fellowship of Evangelical Students. For information about local and regional activities, write Public Relations Dept., InterVarsity Christian Fellowship/USA, 6400 Schroeder Rd., P.O. Box 7895, Madison, WI 53707-7895.

Cover photograph: Erich Schremp/Photo Researchers, Inc.

ISBN 0-8308-1947-9

Printed in the United States of America ♾

Library of Congress Cataloging-in-Publication Data

Schaeffer, Francis A. (Francis August)
    The God who is there / Francis A. Schaeffer.—30th anniversary
ed.
        p.   cm.
    Originally published: Chicago : Inter-Varsity Press, 1968.
    Includes bibliographical references and index.
    ISBN 0-8308-1947-9 (pbk. : alk. paper)
    1. Apologetics. 2. Christianity—20th century.   I. Title.
BT1102.S3   1998
239—dc21   *98-8089*
                                                                             CIP

20	19	18	17	16	15	14	13	12	11	10	9	8	7	6	5	4	3	2	1
15	14	13	12	11	10	09	08	07	06	05	04	03	02	01	00	99	98		

To Edith my wife
Who has walked hand in hand with me
for a very short forty-seven years

Section II: The Relationship of the New Theology to the Intellectual Climate

Today's Opportunity for the New Theology

Section III: How Historic Christianity Differs from the New Theology

---

Section IV: Speaking Historic Christianity into the Twentieth-Century Climate

Acknowledgments

Thanks are due to the following for permission to quote from copyrighted works:
Madame Marguerite Arp for the poem "für Theo van Doesburg" by Hans Arp;

Dylan Thomas, *Collected Poems* © 1957 by New Directions Publishing Corporation.
Reprinted by permission of New Directions Publishing Corporation;

the author and the *New Yorker* for an extract from "Figure in an Imaginary Landscape"
by Calvin Tomkins, © 1964 The New Yorker Magazine Inc.;

Agence Hoffman for an extract from the preface "A Sense of Wonder" by Henry
Miller to *The History of Art* by Elie Favre (in the translation which appeared in *Vogue*,
December 1964);

Dr. John Macquarrie for an extract from an article which appeared in *The Listener*,
April 12, 1962.

Foreword

It is hard to understand how an orthodox, evangelical, Bible-believing Christian can fail to be excited. The answers in the realm of the intellect should make us overwhelmingly excited. But more than this, we are returned to a personal relationship with the God who is there. If we are unexcited as Christians, we should go back and see what is wrong. (p. 190)

The God Who Is There was Francis Schaeffer's first book, but it was not my first introduction to the man.[1] Almost forty years ago, while in graduate school at the University of Missouri, I was puzzling out the relation between my faith and my academic study of English literature. I had found little either in theology or Christian philosophy to help me. Fortunately, I had discovered neoscholastic philosophers like Jacques Maritain and Étienne Gilson, and the Russian intellectual Nikolai Berdyaev. But there was no one whose Christian tradition was close to my own mid-American evangelicalism.

Jay Adams, then a fellow graduate student in speech, said, "You now should read James Orr and Abraham Kuyper. And, most of all, you should get together with Francis Schaeffer. Orr and Kuyper are from a previous generation, but Schaeffer is doing now just what you're interested in." I immediately read Orr and Kuyper and was helped greatly. But Francis Schaeffer, then unpublished and living in Switzerland, was beyond my reach. I promptly forgot about him.

Five or six years later, when I became the editor of InterVarsity Press, two books by Francis Schaeffer were in the publishing pipeline. *Escape from Reason* would have been published first, but its delivery from the British printer was postponed by a strike on the St. Lawrence Seaway. *The God Who Is There* was being printed in the United States, the result being that both books were released in the fall of 1968, just a few days before Schaeffer gave the lectures at Wheaton College that became *Death in the City*.

I vividly remember my first exposure to Schaeffer's ideas. It came the summer of 1968 as I read the British edition of *Escape from Reason*, first half on the train into Chicago from Downers Grove, second half on the return. And I was disappointed. Schaeffer did not understand the Renaissance, I thought. Seventeenth-century English literature was my field. I knew the Renaissance rather well, I thought. But Schaeffer saw a different reality. Then I read *The God Who Is There* and still was disappointed, even making occasional disparaging comments to my colleagues.

It was months later that I realized I had been wrong. I had simply misread Schaeffer. What made the difference was my first full-fledged editing task: *Death in the City*. This required transforming the transcripts of Schaeffer's Wheaton lectures into prose that could be read without the presence of the speaker's voice. Among the many things this project taught me is the marked differences between the idioms of spoken and written English. I had to immerse my mind in the mind of the speaker, think his thoughts after him and recast the sentences. By the time I had finished this process, I knew why my first readings of Schaeffer were so off target. *Death in the City* reshaped my own grasp not just of Jeremiah and Romans, its subjects, but my understanding of *The God Who Is There* and *Escape from Reason* as well.

For many people raised on Schaeffer in the 1960s and 1970s, this recasting was never necessary. Schaeffer spoke their language. They had not been schooled in the traditional language of cultural criticism; they did not know that *rationalism* was a word normally used to describe the philosophy of a limited number of early modern philosophers (Descartes, Spinoza and Leibnitz) and that Locke, Berkeley and Hume were called *empiricists*. Schaeffer referred to all of these and a host of other philosophers as *rationalists*. But Schaeffer by his own explicit definition was not wrong.

Schaeffer defined *rationalism* as "the system whereby men and women, beginning absolutely by themselves, try rationally to build out from themselves, having only Man as their integration point, to find all knowledge, meaning and value" (pp. 29-30). And he consistently used the word in this sense. If I had extended Schaeffer the right to be an original philosopher, I would not have made so many mistakes in my first reading.

So: a caveat to new readers of Schaeffer. Lay aside your presumption that you understand all the terms that he uses. Pay attention to Schaeffer's definitions. I am convinced that you will find him an insightful and original philosopher. Conceptions like "the line of despair," "upper story" and "lower story" are unique to Schaeffer and brilliantly apt. There are, as well, twists on terms like "antithesis" and "dialectical method."

I recall a conversation with another publisher who said he hadn't read Schaeffer himself but that his wife had *The God Who Is There* in one hand and a dictionary in the other. The dictionary would help with words Schaeffer was using in common with the tradition, but she would need to pay attention to Schaeffer's own twist on many of them. Of course, she had one advantage over me: this was probably her first introduction to philosophical theology; her mind was yet to be shaped. My mind had to be reshaped; that's harder.

The God Who Is There for the Twenty-first Century

A new millennium is upon us. Has Schaeffer's thought any relevance to the beginning of the twenty-first century?

Schaeffer has had a tremendous impact on evangelical thought during the last four decades of the twentieth century. It is little exaggeration to say that if Schaeffer had not lived, historians of the future looking back on these decades would have to invent him in order to explain what happened. Moreover, Schaeffer will long be read, studied, imitated *and* transcended. There is no question about that. But I would like to single out five notions whose impact will, I trust, continue to resonate. I will call them *passions*, for that is what they were to Schaeffer and what I would want them to be for my generation and generations of Christians to come. They are a passion for the God who is there, a passion for truth, a compassion for people, a passion for relevant and honest communication, and a passion for Scripture.

A passion for the God who is there. By this I do not, of course, mean the book. I mean passion for direct engagement with him who calls himself I AM. For Schaeffer, God is not the first thought or the first presupposition; he is the first "thing"—Being himself—infinite personal, triune, intelligent, good, loving, engaging. Everything rests on him. Schaeffer began where we all should begin—with God himself. We do not presume to say anything about God he has not revealed about himself. God is God and we are not.

I am convinced that if all our theologies began where Schaeffer's does, we would be far more humble about both ourselves and our theologies. As firm as Schaeffer was in his theological pronounce-ments, he was humble about his own accomplishments and willing to say (I heard him do so) to both his friends and his critics, "Okay. You don't like how I have put this. You think it can be done better. Please, go and do better."

One of the glories of Schaeffer's sermons, lectures and books is that they exude a sense of God. You feel as you read *The God Who Is There* that this man knows the God who is there, not as an abstraction but as one with whom personal encounter characterizes the relationship. Schaeffer did not like the word *encounter* in relation to God because he felt that it suggested an intellectually contentless relationship. But understood as filled with content, *encounter* is the right word. Schaeffer met God, one imagines, daily in devotion and always as the living background motif of all his thoughts and all his encounters with others.

A passion for truth. This doesn't need my documentation. The first sentence of *The God Who Is There* reads: "The present chasm between the generations has been brought about almost entirely by a change in the concept of truth" (p. 25). For the next two hundred pages, Schaeffer rings changes on this motif.

If his analysis was a surprise to evangelicals in the late 1960s, it is no surprise now. Our conception of what we can know has steadily been reduced. Early modernism held that we could know the truth about external reality. Late modernism allowed that we could know models and paradigms that at least assumed there is a determinate reality behind all scientific formulations. Postmodernism has reduced paradigms to language games in which truth becomes, in Richard Rorty's words, "a property of linguistic entities, of sentences."[2] Schaeffer saw this coming. His analysis of the situation in the late sixties fits the nineties too. There has been no change in direction, just a growing sophistication in how life below and above the line of despair continues on its hectic pace.

The need to emphasize the unity of truth, the need to stand against the relativism that says, "Regardless of the content of our beliefs, I'm okay, you're okay, and that's okay": these remain, though the illustrations would be drawn from a fresh body of names. Writing today, Schaeffer would cite Rorty, Michel Foucault, Jacques Derrida, Jean-François Lyotard, Václav Havel and Richard Dawkins. Their names would appear as frequently as the names of Albert Camus, Jean-Paul Sartre, Léopold Sédar Senghor, B. F. Skinner and Francis Crick. But his basic approach would not need to change. Fortunately, many who have been influenced by Schaeffer have continued at least part of the task he set for himself—to understand the culture so that Christians could speak the truth of historic Christianity into the twentieth and now the twenty-first century.

A compassion for people. I could have put this before Schaeffer's passion for truth and just after his passion for God. I have probably been more influenced by this than by any single or group of ideas. Here Schaeffer has shaped my heart, or more accurately, he has modeled a heart for people and has, thereby, encouraged me to let God shape my heart.

Can there be anyone who has read his books or talked with him or heard lectures or observed him answering questions, sometimes from hostile critics, who cannot say, "Here is a man who loved not just humankind but Paul and Mary and John and Bill and every nameless person whom he touched"? Even in his books his compassion shows through both the illustrations he gives and the rhetoric he uses, not just to tell the stories but to explain his ideas. He pictures, for example, two lovers on the left bank of the Seine:

They fall in love and yet cry because they do not believe love exists. If I met any of these, I would put my hand gently on their shoulders and say, "You are separated from God if you do not accept Christ as your Savior, but at this moment you understand something real about the universe. Though your system may say love does not exist, your own experience shows that it does." They have not touched the personal God who exists, but for a fleeting moment they have touched the existence of true personality in their love. (p. 45)

How many of us—evangelists, apologists, philosophers, cultural critics—would think to react like this? There was a deep pastoral touch in all that Schaeffer wrote and did.

Many Schaeffer readers will recognize this illustration, for Schaeffer used it frequently in his talks. I will use it to make two general observations. The first concerns compassion. At St. Andrews University in Scotland, Schaeffer was talking with a peculiarly difficult student.

After only two minutes of talking in his room, he [the student] said, "Sir, I don't think we are communicating." I started again. About two minutes later he repeated himself, "Sir, I don't think we are communicating." I began to think that the half-hour would be spent in a nonsense session! I looked down and saw that he had very thoughtfully prepared a lovely tea. There it all was, pot of tea, cups and so on. So I said rather gruffly to him, "Give me some tea!" He was taken aback, but he passed me a cup, full of tea. Then I said, "Sir, I think we are communicating." From then on we had a very effective conversation. (pp. 123-24)

Notice the description *("very thoughtfully . . . lovely tea"):* odd words for an intellectual apologist. Schaeffer was sensitive to the "mannishness" of the student: first, his sense of taste and (surprising) propriety (tea is almost a ceremony in Britain) and, second, his ability to communicate even if he denied it. Still, to make a point he shocked the student with his own feigned insensitivity. Here is a union of compassion and firmness, of love in the bounds of reason, respect in the bounds of truth.

My second observation about this interchange with the student is that it illustrates his passion for relevant and honest communication. Christian friends of the difficult student had not been able to get a hearing for the gospel. Schaeffer found a way to break through the barriers to communication. He caught the student at a point of tension. The student held communication not to be happening, but he experienced it as happening. Schaeffer cleverly demonstrated to the student that even he knew communication was taking place. So here was an opening for communication not just about communication but about the reality that underlies our experience of communication and about the God who makes communication possible.

I can contrast Schaeffer's dialogue with a conversation I once had in a college lecture hall. Suddenly a student called out, "But communication is impossible." I replied, with considerable wit, I thought, "What?" He said it again, "People can't communicate." I replied, "What?" Again he repeated himself and I did too. At that point he got angry and walked out.

Cleverness is one thing, but it is to be used with caution. Not only did I lose the "audience" with the student, but I discovered as well that others in the room did not understand what had happened. They were then lost to me as well. Schaeffer himself had an experience similar to mine, though it was prompted by a student, not himself.

Here is Schaeffer's own cautionary words about pushing people to the logic of their presuppositions:

> This is not a game I am playing. If I begin to enjoy it as a kind of intellectual exercise, then I am cruel and can expect no real spiritual results. As I push the man off his false balance, he must be able to feel that I care for him. Otherwise I will only end up destroying him, and the cruelty and ugliness of it all will destroy me as well. (p. 156)

If we at the beginning of the twenty-first century have only one thing to learn from Schaeffer, let it be compassion for people.

A passion for culture. Some people might choose this as *the* defining feature of Francis Schaeffer. Others have a passion for truth and a compassion for people. Schaeffer combined that with a passion for understanding the contemporary context in which both truth and people fit. To love people and speak the truth one has to know the culture.

My memory of working with Schaeffer played me false as I began the task of rereading *The God Who Is There.* Having heard many of his lectures, and having edited a dozen of his books, including *How Should We Then Live?* and *Whatever Happened to the Human Race?* I found less cultural commentary in *The God Who Is There* than I had remembered. Much of it consists of thumbnail sketches of high points in the life and works of various philosophers, intellectuals, painters, writers and composers. Readers not familiar with the figures he discusses may be confused.

Some who are familiar with the figures he discusses may say that Schaeffer has not understood them. I thought so on first reading. But when one holds off the criticism until one understands what Schaeffer is looking at and what he has focused attention on, and goes back to the figures themselves to confirm one's views, Schaeffer's analysis often strikes home. Certainly he had a wide exposure to Western art and must have haunted museums. In much of his writing, the insights of art historian Hans Rookmaaker, his close friend and colleague, provided ballast for Schaeffer's comments. When he goes into detail, his remarks can be especially apt. Take for instance his treatment of John Cage (pp. 95, 97-99).

The point of Schaeffer's cultural critique is not, of course, to produce an academic analysis. It is rather to explain to those who were living through the sixties and seventies just what was influencing their thoughts and lifestyles, whether they knew it or not. On this score, his work is masterful.

The thumbnail sketches have inspired me to look differently at art works, to see what I hadn't seen and to continue the process over the years. Schaeffer would have liked that, even if I came up with conclusions that would differ from his. Of course, with his emphasis on antithesis, if our views contradicted each other, at least one of them had to be false!

A passion for relevant and honest communication. Schaeffer had an uncanny and I think intuitive ability to communicate to both intellectuals and ordinary people of his day. In his books and lectures he emphasized that evangelical Christians needed to know how and what the world thinks, and then to address the world with a relevant message. He called this "speaking historic Christianity into the twentieth century." The relevance of Christian rhetoric to the contemporary mind is crucial.

I taught English literature in college for over ten years. I thought I knew how to communicate with students concerning cultural issues. The day after the shooting of four students at Kent State University in May 1970, my college, Northern Illinois University, was in chaos. I found myself trying to explain to a class on John Milton what was going on. My own academically informed language was not getting through. Without telling the class what I was doing, I changed my analysis to the terminology of Schaeffer. Suddenly eyes began to light up. One student said, "If we had other classes like this, we wouldn't be rioting." Another asked, "Have you ever heard of Francis Schaeffer?" This student had learned of his work through the local Methodist Student Center. Schaeffer had done what he set out to do.

But Schaeffer was not only interested in relevant communication. He was interested in honest communication as well. Among the important contributions Schaeffer made to good thinking in general is to unmask the way language is used by modern intellectuals, theologians and cultural commentators.

Schaeffer would probably not like to be thought of as one of the hermeneuts of suspicion, but he performed for Christians a task much like theirs when he identified and gave examples of *semantic mysticism*. Words are often used to mask reality, to transform ideas about it into palatable form. Words like *love*, for instance, were then and still are being used for what is actually only raw physical sexual activity. "I *love* you" often means, more honestly, "I want to *sleep with* you," or something even cruder.

Schaeffer's unmasking of the word *pantheism* is especially apt:

Though it [pantheism] speaks of something absolutely and finally impersonal, yet the *theism* part of the word causes a reaction of acceptance, since *theism* carries overtones of personality. Now suppose you were to substitute the word *pan-everythingism* (which is what it really means). The whole reaction would be different. (p. 79)

Think about it. My first reaction was *No, you're wrong. A pantheist believes that all of nature is divine; that it is indeed god.* But that's exactly Schaeffer's point. The word *god* functions as if personality were involved. In the sort of pantheism Schaeffer is talking about (Advaita-

Vedanta Hinduism or Zen Buddhism, for example), there is no personality involved. That has been left behind. Even to say it has been transcended would be semantic mysticism because the word *transcendent* has in our culture a profoundly theistic sense. Better to say the Void (but then the capital on *void* functions as semantic mysticism) or that ultimately reality is pure energy without differentiation (but even energy has differentiation). Better yet to say, think or do nothing to address or describe ultimate reality.

With this kind of critique, the whole of language could be seen to mask reality, to conceal plays for power, in short, to be subject to total deconstruction. But Schaeffer's critique is rooted in "the God who is there" who speaks a Word that is both personally and propositionally true. A God who in Scripture spoke words that name the world as the world really is.

A passion for Scripture. This passion shows through all of Schaeffer's writings, lectures and sermons. In *The God Who Is There* this is both stated and operative as an underlying motif. God has spoken truly. The Scriptures are the propositional, verbalized revelation of God. All the presuppositions with which Schaeffer approaches his work are drawn from the Scriptures, so far as he understands them.

Nonetheless, with all his emphasis on the truthfulness of Scripture, with all the explicit use he makes of Scripture as the justification for his views, with all his concern for orthodoxy, he knew that the Scriptures were not the final thing.

> The Bible, the historic Creeds and orthodoxy are important because God is there, and, finally, that is the only reason that they have their importance. (p. 177)

Given this and the intellectual satisfaction that comes when the mind is in tune with the God who is there, "it is hard to understand how an orthodox, evangelical, Bible-believing Christian can fail to be excited" (p. 190).

This book has precisely the right title. It is a penetrating, magnificent, wise book by a man who knew then, and now knows more fully, though perhaps not even yet exhaustively, "the God who is there."

James W. Sire

Section 1

The Intellectual &
Cultural Climate
of the Second Half
of the Twentieth
Century

Thou didst create all things,
and by thy will they existed and were created.
  (Revelation 4:11 RSV)

So God created man in his own image, in the image of God
he created him; male and female he created them.
  (Genesis 1:27 RSV)

But now thus says the LORD,
  he who created you, O Jacob,
  he who formed you, O Israel:
"Fear not, for I have redeemed you;
  I have called you by name, you are mine;
When you pass through the waters I will be with you;
  and through the rivers, they shall not overwhelm you;
when you walk through fire you shall not be burned,
  and the flame shall not consume you.
For I am the LORD your God,
  the Holy One of Israel, your Savior."
  (Isaiah 43:1-3 RSV)

The universe was not pregnant with life nor the biosphere with man. Our number came up in a Monte Carlo game.
  (JACQUES MONOD)

To man qua man we readily say good riddance.
  (B. F. SKINNER)

1
The Gulf
Is Fixed

Before the Chasm

The present chasm between the generations has been brought about almost entirely by a change in the concept of truth.

Wherever you look today, the new concept holds the field. The consensus about us is almost monolithic, whether you review the arts, literature or simply read the newspapers and magazines such as *Time*, *Life*, *Newsweek*, *The Listener* or *The Observer*. On every side you can feel the stranglehold of this new methodology—and by "methodology" we mean the way we approach truth and knowing. It is like suffocating in a particularly bad London fog. And just as fog cannot be kept out by walls or doors, so this consensus comes in around us, until the room we live in is no longer unpolluted, and yet we hardly realize what has happened.

The tragedy of our situation today is that men and women are being fundamentally affected by the new way of looking at truth, and yet they have never even analyzed the drift which has taken place. Young people from Christian homes are brought up in the old framework of truth. Then they are subjected to the modern framework. In time they become confused because they do not understand the alternatives with which they are being presented. Confusion becomes bewilderment, and before long they are overwhelmed. This is unhappily true not only of young people, but of many pastors, Christian educators, evangelists and missionaries as well.

So this change in the concept of the way we come to knowledge and truth is the most crucial problem, as I understand it, facing Christianity today.

If you had lived in Europe, let us say prior to about 1890, or in the United States before about 1935, you would not have had to spend much time, in practice, in thinking about your presuppositions. (These dates are arbitrary as the change came, in Europe at least, fairly gradually. In America the crucial years of change were from 1913 to 1940, and during these relatively few years the whole way of thinking underwent a revolution; 1913 was a most important year in the United States, not because it was the year before the First World War, but for another highly significant reason, as we shall see later.)

Before these dates everyone would have been working on much the same presuppositions, which in practice seemed to accord with the Christian's own presuppositions. This was true both in the area of epistemology and methodology. *Epistemology* is the theory of how we know, or how we can be sure that what we think we know of the world about us is correct. *Methodology* is how we approach the question of truth and knowing.

Now it may be argued that the non-Christians had no right to act on the presuppositions they acted on. That is true. They were being romantic in accepting optimistic answers without a sufficient base. Nevertheless they went on thinking and acting as if these presuppositions were true.

What were these presuppositions? The basic one was that there really are such things as absolutes. They accepted the possibility of an absolute in the area of Being (or *knowledge*), and in the area of *morals*. Therefore, because they accepted the possibility of absolutes, though people might have disagreed as to what these were, nevertheless they could reason together on the classical basis of antithesis. They took it for granted that if anything was true, the opposite was false. In morality, if one thing was right, its opposite was wrong. This little formula, "A is A" and "If you have A, it is not non-A," is the first move in classical logic. If you understand the extent to which this no longer holds sway, you will understand our present situation.

Absolutes imply antithesis. The non-Christian went on romantically operating on this basis without a sufficient cause, an adequate base, for doing so. Thus it was still possible to discuss what was right and wrong, what was true and false. One could tell a non-Christian to "be a good girl" and, while she might not have followed your advice, at least she would have understood what you were talking about. To say the same thing to a truly modern girl today would be to make a "nonsense" statement. The blank look you might receive would not mean that your standards had been rejected, but that your message was meaningless.

The shift has been tremendous. Thirty or more years ago you could have said such things as "This is true" or "This is right," and you would have been on everybody's wavelength. People may or may not have thought out their beliefs consistently, but everyone would have been talking to each other as though the idea of antithesis was correct. Thus in evangelism, in spiritual matters and in Christian education, you could have begun with the certainty that your audience understood you.

Presuppositional Apologetics Would Have Stopped the Decay

It was indeed unfortunate that our Christian "thinkers," in the time before the shift took place and the chasm was fixed, did not teach and preach with a clear grasp of presuppositions.[1] Had they done this they would not have been taken by surprise, and they could have helped young people to face their difficulties. The really foolish thing is that even now, years after the shift is complete, many Christians still do not know what is happening. And this is because they are still not being taught the importance of thinking in terms of presuppositions, especially concerning truth.

The floodwaters of secular thought and liberal theology overwhelmed the church because the leaders did not understand the importance of combating a false set of presuppositions. They largely fought the battle on the wrong ground and so, instead of being ahead in both defense and communication, they lagged woefully behind. This was a real weakness which it is hard, even today, to rectify among evangelicals.

The use of classical apologetics before this shift took place was effective only because non-Christians were functioning, on the surface, on the same presuppositions, even if they had an inadequate base for them. In classical apologetics though, presuppositions were rarely analyzed, discussed or taken into account.

So if a man got up to preach the gospel and said, "Believe this, it is true," those who heard would have said, "Well, if that is so, then its opposite is false." The presupposition of antithesis pervaded men's entire mental outlook. We must not forget that historic Christianity stands on a basis of antithesis. Without it historic Christianity is meaningless. The basic antithesis is that God objectively exists in contrast (in antithesis) to his not existing. Which of these two are the reality, changes everything in the area of knowledge and morals and in the whole of life.

The Line of Despair

Thus we have a date line like this:

	Europe before 1890 and the U.S. before 1935
The line of despair ——————	
	Europe after 1890 U.S. after 1935

Notice that I call the line, the line of despair. Above this line we find men living with their romantic notions of absolutes (though with no sufficient logical basis). This side of the line, all is changed. Man thinks differently concerning truth.

In order to understand this line of despair more clearly, think of it not as a simple horizontal line but as a staircase:

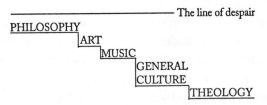

Each of the steps represents a certain stage in time. The higher is earlier, the lower later. It was in this order that the shift in truth affected men's lives.

The shift spread gradually, and in three different ways. People did not suddenly wake up one morning and find that it had permeated everywhere at once.

First of all it spread geographically. The ideas began in Germany and spread outward. They affected the Continent first, then crossed the Channel to England, and then the Atlantic to America. Second, it spread through society, from the real intellectual to the more educated, down to the workers, reaching the middle class last of all. Third, it spread as represented in the diagram, from one discipline to another, beginning with the philosophers and ending with the theologians. Theology has been last for a long time. It is curious to me, in studying this whole cultural drift, that so many pick up the latest theological fashion and hail it as something new. *But in fact, what the new theology is now saying has already been said previously in each of the other disciplines.*

It is important to grasp the fundamental nature of this line. If Christians try to talk to people as though they were above the line when in reality they are this side of it, we will only beat the air. This goes as much for dockers as for intellectuals. The same holds true for the concept of spirituality. This side of the line, "spirituality" becomes exactly opposite to Christian spirituality.

Unity and Disunity in Rationalism

There is a real unity in non-Christian thought, as well as differences within that unity. The shift to moving below the line of despair is one of the differences within the unity of non-Christian thought. The unifying factor can be called rationalism, or if you prefer, humanism— though if we use the latter term, we must be careful to distinguish its meaning in this context from the more limited sense of the word *humanism* in such a book as *The Humanist Frame,*[2] edited by Sir Julian Huxley. This latter kind of humanism has become a technical term within the larger meaning of the word. Humanism in the larger, more inclusive sense is the system whereby men and women, beginning absolutely by themselves, try rationally to build out from themselves, having only Man as their integration point, to find all knowledge, meaning and value. We must also ensure that the word *rationalism,* which means the same thing as humanism in the wider sense, is not confused with the word *rational. Rational* means that the things which are about us are not contrary to reason; or, to put it another way, man's aspiration of reason is valid. And so the Judeo-Christian position is rational, but it is the very antithesis of rationalism.

So rationalism or humanism is the unity within non-Christian thought. Yet if Christians are going to be able to understand and talk to people in their generation, they must take account of the form rationalism is currently taking. In one way it is always the same—people trying to build from themselves alone. In another sense it is constantly shifting, with different emphases with which a Christian must be acquainted if he is not equipping himself to work in a period which no longer exists.

The line of despair indicates a titanic shift at this present time within the unity of rationalism. Above the line, people were rationalistic optimists. They believed they could begin with themselves and draw a circle which would encompass all thoughts of life and life itself without having to depart from the logic of antithesis. They thought that on their own, rationalistically, finite people could find a unity within the total diversity—an adequate explanation for the whole of reality. This is where philosophy stood prior to our own era. The only real argument between these rationalistic optimists concerned what circle should be drawn. One person would draw a circle and say, "You can live within this circle." The next person would cross it out and would draw a different circle. The next person would come along and, crossing out the previous circle, draw his own—*ad infinitum.* So if you start to study philosophy by pursuing the *history* of philosophy, by the time you are through with all these circles, each one of which has been destroyed by the next, you may feel like jumping off London Bridge!

But at a certain point this attempt to spin out a *unified* optimistic humanism came to an end. The philosophers came to the conclusion that they were not going to find a unified rationalistic circle that would contain all thought, and in which they could live. It was as though the rationalist suddenly realized that he was trapped in a large round room with no doors and no windows, nothing but complete darkness. From the middle of the room he would feel his way to the walls and begin to look for an exit. He would go round the circumference, and then the terrifying truth would dawn on him that there was no exit, no exit at all! *In the end the philosophers came to the realization that they could not find this unified rationalistic circle and so, departing from the classical methodology of antithesis, they shifted the concept of truth, and modern man was born.*

In this way modern man moved under the line of despair. He was driven to it against his desire. He remained a rationalist, but he had changed. Do we Christians understand this shift in the contemporary world? If we do not understand it, then we are largely talking to ourselves.

Tendency Towards a Uniform Culture

The importance of understanding the chasm to which man's thinking has brought him is not of intellectual value alone but of spiritual value as well. The Christian is to resist the spirit of the world. But when we say this, we must understand that the world-spirit does not always take the same form. So the Christian must resist the spirit of the world *in the form it takes in his own generation.* If he does not do this, he is not resisting the spirit of the world at all. This is especially so for our generation, as the forces at work against us are of such a total nature. It is our generation of Christians more than any other who need to heed these words attributed to Martin Luther:

If I profess with the loudest voice and clearest exposition every portion of the truth of God except precisely that little point which the world and the devil are at that moment attacking, I am not confessing Christ, however boldly I may be professing Christ. Where the battle rages, there the loyalty of the soldier is proved, and to be steady on all the battlefield besides, is mere flight and disgrace if he flinches at that point.

It would be false to say that there is a totally uniform culture. This is not so. And yet as we study the art and literature of the past and those things which help us to understand a culture, we find that there tends to be a drift towards a monolithic and uniform whole.

Through a study of archaeology it is possible to show how a certain idea developed in one place and then over a period of several hundred years spread over wide areas. One could give as an example the Indo-European culture, whose spread can be traced through the flow of certain words.

In the distant past it took so long for cultural concepts to spread that by the time they had reached other areas they had sometimes already changed at their place of origin. But today the world is small, and it is very possible to have a monolithic culture spreading rapidly and influencing great sections of mankind. No artificial barriers, such as the Iron Curtain, can keep out the flow of these ideas. As the world has shrunk, and as it has largely become post-Christian, both sides of the Iron Curtain have followed the same methodology and the same basic monolithic thought-form—namely, the lack of absolutes and antithesis, leading to pragmatic relativism.

In our modern forms of specialized education there is a tendency to lose the whole in the parts, and in this sense we can say that our generation produces few truly educated people. True education means thinking by associating across the various disciplines, and not just being highly qualified in one field, as a technician might be. I suppose no discipline has tended to think more in fragmented fashion than the orthodox or evangelical theology of today.

Those standing in the stream of historic Christianity have been especially slow to understand the relationships between various areas of thought. When the apostle warned us to "keep [ourselves] unspotted from the world,"[3] he was not talking of some abstraction. If the Christian is to apply this injunction to himself he must understand what confronts him antagonistically in his own moment of history. Otherwise he simply becomes a useless museum piece and not a living warrior for Jesus Christ.

The orthodox Christian has paid a very heavy price, both in the defense and communication of the gospel, for his failure to think and act as an educated person understanding and at war with the uniformity of our modern culture.

2

The First Step in the Line of Despair

Philosophy

Hegel, the Doorway

It was the German philosopher Hegel (1770-1831) who became the man to open the door into the line of despair. Before his time truth was conceived on the basis of antithesis, not for any adequate reason but because man romantically acted upon it.

This book is not intended to be exhaustive in its treatment of the developments from the time of the Renaissance leading up to Hegel. *Escape from Reason* gives a more complete resumé of the developments from Aquinas, through the Renaissance, the birth of modern science, and including the place of Immanuel Kant. Kant is most important, and to omit him would leave out one of the key pieces in the development of modern thought.

Truth, in the sense of antithesis, is related to the idea of cause and effect. Cause and effect produces a chain reaction which goes straight on in a horizontal line. With the coming of Hegel this changed.

We must understand the importance of timing. What Hegel taught arrived at just the right moment of history for his thinking to have its maximum effect.

Imagine that Hegel was sitting one day in the local tavern, surrounded by his friends, conversing on the philosophical issues of the day. Suddenly he put down his mug of beer on the table and said, "I have a new idea. From now on let us think in this way: instead of thinking in terms of cause and effect, what we really have is a thesis, and opposite it an antithesis, with the answer to their relationship not a horizontal movement of cause and effect, but a synthesis." Now suppose also that a hard-headed German businessman had been standing by and had overheard his remark. He might have thought, "How abstruse and impractical!" But he could not have been further from the truth. Because whether Hegel himself or those listening understood it to be the case, when Hegel propounded this idea he changed the world.

It has never been the same since. Among other things, the concept of dialectical thinking was based on this idea, and it was, and is, crucial to Marxism. By our era Hegelian synthesis dominates on both sides of the Iron Curtain.

If one understands the development of philosophy, or morals, or political thought from that day to this, one knows that Hegel and synthesis have won. In other words, Hegel has removed the straight line of previous thought, and in its place he has substituted a triangle. Instead of antithesis we have, as modern man's approach to truth, synthesis. Hegel did not put it this simply. His thinking and writing are complicated, but the conclusion is that all possible positions are relativized, and leads to the concept that truth is to be sought in synthesis rather than antithesis.

But notice, Hegel was only a door to the line of despair. He himself never went below it. A good case can be made from his writings for classifying him as an idealist in that he tried to solve the problem of unity with his religious language. He thought that in practice synthesis could be arrived at by reason. But this did not prove possible, and so the next man we have to consider went below the line.

Kierkegaard, the First Man Below

It is often said that Søren Kierkegaard, the Dane (1813-1855), is the father of all modern thinking. And so he is. He is the father of modern existential thinking, both secular and theological thinking. Our diagram now looks like this:

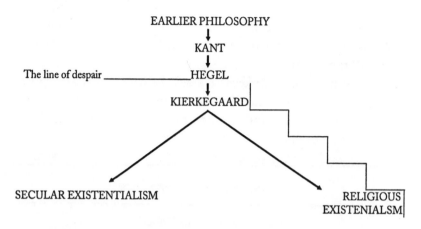

Why is it that Kierkegaard can so aptly be thought of as the father of both? What proposition did he add to the flow of thought that made the difference? Kierkegaard led to the conclusion that you could not arrive at synthesis by reason. Instead, you achieve everything of real importance by a leap of faith.

Kierkegaard was a complex man, and his writings, especially his devotional writings, are often very helpful. For example, the Bible-believing Christians in Denmark still use these devotional writings. We can also be totally sympathetic to his outcry about the deadness of much of the Church in his day. However, in his more philosophical writings he did become the father of modern thought. This turns upon his writing of Abraham and the "sacrifice" of Isaac. Kierkegaard said this was an act of faith with nothing rational to base it on or to which to relate it. Out of this came the modern concept of a "leap of faith" and the total separation of the rational and faith.

In this thinking concerning Abraham, Kierkegaard had not read the Bible carefully enough. Before Abraham was asked to move toward the sacrifice of Isaac (which, of course, God did not allow to be consummated), he had much propositional revelation from God, he had seen God, God had fulfilled promises to him. In short,

God's words at this time were in the context of Abraham's strong reasons for knowing that God both existed and was totally trustworthy.

This does not minimize Abraham's faith shown in the long march to Mt. Moriah and all the rest, but it certainly was not a "leap of faith" separated from rationality.

I do not think that Kierkegaard would be happy, or would agree, with that which has developed from his thinking in either secular or religious existentialism. But what he wrote gradually led to the absolute separation of the rational and logical from faith.

The reasonable and faith bear no relationship to each other, like this:

FAITH (NONREASON—OPTIMISM)

THE RATIONAL (PESSIMISM)

It is not our purpose here to discuss all that Kierkegaard taught. There was much more than this. *But the important thing about him is that when he put forth the concept of a leap of faith, he became in a real way the father of all modern existential thought, both secular and theological.*

As a result of this, from that time on, if rationalistic man wants to deal with the really important things of human life (such as purpose, significance, the validity of love), he must discard rational thought about them and make a gigantic, nonrational leap of faith. The rationalistic framework had failed to produce an answer on the basis of reason, and so all hope of a uniform field of knowledge had to be abandoned. We get the resulting dichotomy like this:

THE NONRATIONAL AND NONLOGICAL	Existential experience; the final experience; the first-order experience
THE RATIONAL AND LOGICAL	Only particulars, no purpose, no meaning. Man is a machine.

Once we appreciate the development of modern philosophy in this way, we may note that though there appear to be many forms of philosophy today, in reality there are very few. They have a uniform cast about them. For example, if you listened to the defining philosophy as taught in Cambridge, and then turn to the existentialism of, say, Karl Jaspers, you might think there was no unity between them. But this is not so. There is one basic agreement in almost all of the chairs of philosophy today, and that is a radical denial of the possibility of drawing a circle which will encompass all. In this sense the philosophies of today can be called in all seriousness antiphilosophies.

The Existentialism of Jaspers, Sartre and Heidegger

In the two halves of existential thinking which we said flowed from Kierkegaard, we will pick up first that of the secular. Later we will pick up the theological existentialism in considering Karl Barth.

There are three main schools of secular existentialist thinking: the Swiss, the French and the German. Most people do not know the work of Karl Jaspers (1883-1969) in Switzerland as well as that of his French or German contemporaries, but he is an exceedingly important man. He is German, but taught at the University of Basel. He placed a great deal of emphasis on the need to wait for a nonrational "final experience," which, he said, would give meaning to life. People who follow Jaspers have come to me and said, "I have had a final experience." They never expect me to ask them what it was. The simple fact is that if I asked such a thing, it would prove that I was among the uninitiated.

To describe it as an *existential* experience means that it cannot be communicated. It is not possible to communicate content with regard to the experience which they have had. Some of these men have sat down with me and said, "It is obvious from looking at you and talking to you, from noticing your sensitivity and sympathy to others, and the openness of your approach to men, that you too are a man who knows the reality of final experience." They mean this as a supreme compliment, and I always say, "Thank you very much indeed." And I mean it, because it is quite remarkable to have one of these men say to an orthodox Christian that they think he understands. But then I go on to say to them, "Yes, I have had a final experience, but it can be verbalized, and it is of a nature that can be rationally discussed." Then

I talk of my personal relationship with the personal God who is there. I try to make them understand that this relationship is based on God's written, propositional communication to men, and on the finished work of Jesus Christ in space-time history. They reply that this is impossible, that I am trying to do something that cannot be done. The discussion goes on from there.

Try to put yourself for a moment in such a man's place. He has a deep problem, for he hangs everything to do with his certainty of being and the hope of significance upon some titanic experience he has had at a specific point in the past.

It would be wrong to imagine that these men are not serious. I wish many evangelicals had the integrity these men show in their struggles. I have been told that when Karl Jaspers began his lectures to his best students he warned them that they must not commit suicide, because it cannot be certain that one has a final experience by taking one's own life. Perhaps we might wish that many Christians who say they believe in Christ had such intensity of commitment.

But in their struggles there is a horror of great darkness. Though they may be people of great sincerity, this does not of itself make them able to communicate to others their experience. Nor can the individual verbalize to himself what has happened. Tomorrow morning they may say, "Yesterday I had an experience." The day after they still say, "I had an experience." A month and a year later they are hanging on grimly to their only hope of significance and certainty of being by repeating, "I know I had an experience." The horror of this situation is due to their putting their hope in a nonrational, nonlogical, noncommunicable experience.

If we move from Switzerland and to French existentialism, we come to Jean-Paul Sartre (1905-1980) and Albert Camus (1913-1960). They differ from one another and yet share the same basic concepts. Sartre, perhaps, speaks the more consistently of the two. He says that we live in an absurd universe. The total, he says, is ridiculous. Nevertheless, you try to authenticate yourself by an act of the will. It does not really matter in which direction you act as long as you act.

Let us take the field of morals as a good example of the direction of his thought. You see an old lady, and if you help her safely across the road you have "authenticated yourself." But if instead you choose to beat her over the head and snatch her handbag, you would equally have "authenticated yourself." The content is unimportant; you just choose and act. That is it; you have authenticated yourself. This is existentialism in its French form. As I shall show later, neither Sartre nor Camus was able to live this out in practice, but it was their theoretical position.

How is it that these men get to such a strange and desperate position? It is because they have gone below the line of despair. They have given up the hope of a rational circle to give an answer to life, and are left with only the antirational.

Finally we have the German form of existentialism, as it was propounded by Martin Heidegger (1889-1976). The fascinating thing about Heidegger is that there are two distinct periods in his life. The first period takes him up to the age of about seventy, and the second from then on. Some of my students have joked about this and made up a song about how "The old Heidegger is the new Heidegger!" The change came because he could no longer live on the basis of his system. Before the change, which we will consider more closely later, Heidegger was a true existentialist. He came to the same need for authentication as Sartre. How was this to be achieved? Not by an act of the *will*, but by a vague *feeling* of dread. Dread is not to be confused with fear. To him fear had an object; dread had not. Authentication comes through feeling the dread, *angst*, of something that is beyond your comprehension—a foreboding, and that is all.

The Antiphilosophy of the Anglo-Saxon World
Two main types of philosophy have recently held the field in the Anglo-Saxon world. They are logical positivism and defining philosophy. Neither of these is rooted in existentialism; indeed both would claim to differ sharply from existentialism. They would strongly insist that they are logical and rational. While we would concede that they are not related in origin to existentialism, nevertheless they have this in common: in their different ways they are all antiphilosophies.

Logical positivism claims to lay the foundation for each step as it goes along, in a rational way. Yet in reality it puts forth no theoretical universal to validate its very first step. Positivists accept (though they present no logical reason why this should be so) that what reaches them from the "outside" may be called "data"; i.e., it has objective validity.

This dilemma was well illustrated by a young man who had been studying logical positivism at Oxford. He was with us in Switzerland as a student in Farel House, and he said one day, "I'm confused about some of these things. I would like to lead a seminar and see how this whole matter stands." So he did. When he began he said, "Well, when this data reaches you . . ." At once I said, "How do you know, on the basis of logical positivism, that it is data?"

He started again, and went on for another sentence or two, and then said a second time, "When this data reaches you . . ." I felt very much that I was slapping a child's hands when it reaches over into the box of chocolates; but I had to say, "No, you must not use the word *data*. It is loaded with all kinds of meaning; it assumes there is objectivity, and your system has never proved it."

"What do I say then?" he replied.

So I said, "Just say blip. You don't know what you mean by data, so substitute blip."

He began once more, "When blip reaches you . . . " and the discussion was over. On the basis of their form of rationalism, there is just as much logic in calling something "blip" as "data."

Thus in its own way, though it uses the title of positivism and operates using reason, it is just as much a leap of faith as existentialism—since it has no postulated circle within which to act which validates reason nor gives a certainty that what we think is data is indeed data.

Michael Polanyi's (1891-1976) work showed the weakness of all forms of "positivism," and today positivism in theory is dead. However, it must be said that the materialistic, rationalistic scientists have shut their eyes to its demise and continue to build their work upon it as though it were alive and well. They are doing their materialistic science with no epistemological base. In the crucial area of knowing, they are not operating on facts but faith.

However, the defining philosophy is more important in England and the United States today.

The starting-point of those who subscribe to this philosophy is, as the title suggests, definition. They say they will on no account take any first step without rationally and logically defining the terms they use. And they will go no further than can be accurately defined.

This is all very well, but even if we overlook the differences in their own ranks as to whether their categories are accurate or not, they still have other problems. Many of them would agree that all their work is no more than *prolegomena*—that is, preparation for philosophy. They start off by defining terms in the hope that one day some of the random pieces may be fitted together. Now this is helpful insofar as they have demonstrated that some problems cease to exist when they have carefully defined the terms involved. In providing a tool for careful thinking, their work has also been most helpful. But they are carefully defining terms without dealing with meaning and purpose. Classical philosophy up through Kant consisted of two parts. It dealt, certainly, with details. But the details were to be set within a circle which, it was claimed, could contain all knowledge and life. But defining philosophy deals with the details only. It would not claim to be a system. In this sense, as a contrast to classical philosophy, it is an antiphilosophy. In it language leads to neither values nor facts, but only to language.

Then second, many of these men also have their own personal leap of faith. As defining philosophers, they have a prestige in their own field. At the same time many of them take a strong position for optimistic humanism.[1] That is, many of them would make the same optimistic statements as a man like Sir Julian Huxley. But what they are doing is this: they are using their prestige as instructors in the art of defining philosophy in order to enhance the strength of their humanistic view regarding man. But it should be observed that weight of scholarship in defining words does not make up for weakness of argument in the larger questions. In fact, there is no bridge at all between their limited philosophy, which says nothing about meaning or purpose, and their optimistic statements. They have leaped over the gap between the two by faith. However careful and rational their definitions of words may be, their observation of man, in that it is optimistic humanism, is unadulterated faith.

And the evolutionary humanism as a whole, which is current today, is in the same plight. Anyone can assert with all the persuasion at his command that mankind can expect a rosy future. But this again is a leap of faith if there is no point of observation, either clinically or sociologically, to demonstrate that man will be better tomorrow than he was yesterday or is today.

Sir Julian Huxley has taken such a purely optimistic answer one step further by stating that man will only be improved by accepting a new mystique. Thus he suggests that society will function better if it has a religion, even though no god really exists.[2] For example, he says:

> From the specifically religious point of view, the desirable direction of evolution might be defined as the divinisation of existence—but for this to have operative significance we must frame a new definition of "the divine" free from all connotations of external supernatural beings.
>
> Religion today is imprisoned in a theistic frame of ideas, compelled to operate in the unrealities of the dualistic world. In the unitary humanist frame it acquires a new look and new freedom. With the aid of our new vision it has the opportunity of escaping from the theistic impasse and of playing its proper role in the real world of unitary existence.

Now it may be true that it can be shown by observation that society copes better with life through believing that there is a god. But in that case, surely optimistic humanism is essentially unreasonable (and, like the others we have discussed, shows exactly the same irrational leap of faith) if in order to be optimistic, its optimism rests upon the necessity of mankind's believing and functioning upon a lie.

The Use of Drugs

It is not only the existentialist who has talked about an experience as a means of validating oneself. Right up to the time of his death Aldous Huxley suggested that a way of achieving what he described as a "first-order experience" would be through drugs.[3] This experience would, like the final experience advocated by the existentialists, be above the line of rational validation, in this way:

THE NONRATIONAL AND NONLOGICAL	A first-order experience by the use of drugs.
THE RATIONAL AND LOGICAL	No purpose or meaning found.

This overwhelming desire for some nonrational experience was responsible for most of the serious use of the drugs LSD and STP in the 1960s. For the sensitive person, drugs were then not usually used for escape. On the contrary, he hoped that by taking them he would experience the reality of something which would give his life some meaning. Intriguingly enough, Professor Timothy Leary, formerly of Harvard University, linked up the LSD experience with that described in the *Tibetan Book of the Dead.*[4] Thus he shows that the desire for, and the form of, this experience changes very little from West to East. Whether it is the existentialist speaking, or Aldous Huxley, or Eastern mysticism, we find a uniform need for an irrational experience to make some sense of life. Their views have brought them to a wall, and by an unrelated leap of faith they hope to clear the wall. Each of their views may be distinguished in detailed description, but they have come to the same wall and are making the same attempt to clear it. Each case involves a nonrational leap of faith.

The chairs of philosophy in most universities have come under the line of despair. The living philosophical discussions have tended to move into unusual settings—such as philosophic astronomy, modern jazz or among the counterculture. It is in such fields that philosophy is being hammered out. Academic philosophy as such, including Anglo-Saxon philosophy, has tended to be antiphilosophy.

In concluding this section let us note that when we speak of being under the line of despair, we do not mean that these people necessarily sit down and weep, but that they have given up all hope of achieving a rational, unified answer to knowledge and life.

What Does and Does Not Happen in These Experiences

It is obvious that often when a man claims to have had an experience, whether under drugs or not, something has certainly happened to him. When he experiences, for example, the "redness" of a red rose, he has really touched something. But what?

Usually only two live options are presented as to what happens in an Eastern religious experience, an existential experience, or a drug experience. One is told either that they have stumbled on "nothing" in their experience, or else that they have met "the reality of god." This latter is especially true when the Eastern religious experience is under consideration. The *guru* says, "I have met something." Usually people describe it as nonsense or say that he has "met God."

The built-in trouble with all these existential experiences is that the content of such an experience is not open to communication. Only the unknowing would demand, "Please describe to me in normal categories what you have experienced."

But I believe that there is a third live option when we ask ourselves what these people have touched. It is an alternative explanation Christians are able to give because we see these people *as they really are* in God's universe.

God has created a real, external world. It is not an extension of his essence. That real, external world exists. God has also created man as a real, personal being, and he possesses a "mannishness" from which he can never escape. On the basis of their own worldview often these experience-seekers are neither sure the external world is there, nor that man as man is there. But I have come to the conclusion that despite their intellectual doubts, many of them *have had* a true experience of the reality of the external world that exists, and/or the "mannishness" that exists. They can do this precisely because this is how God has made man, in his own image, able to experience the real world and man's "mannishness." Thus they have hit upon something which exists, and it is neither nothing, nor is it God. We might sum up this third alternative by saying that when they experience the "redness" of the rose, they are having the experience of the external world, as is the farmer who plows his field. They are both touching the world that is.

In the same way, lovers on the left bank of the Seine in Paris experience the "mannishness" of man when they fall in love and yet cry because they do not believe love exists. If I met any of these, I would put my hand gently on their shoulders and say, "You are separated from God if you do not accept Christ as your Savior, but at this moment you understand something real about the universe. Though your system may say love does not exist, your own experience shows that it does." They have not touched the personal God who exists, but for a fleeting moment they have touched the existence of true personality in their love. This is indeed an objective reality, because God has made their personalities in this way. It is true that in these experiences man has touched something, not nothing; but what he has touched is not God, but the objective reality of the external world and the "mannishness" of man that God has created.

Some have wondered why Christians should not use drugs since drugs are said to sharpen perception. But the price paid for increased perception is much too great. A while ago an anonymous poem was published in the *Listener* based on the 23rd Psalm. It began:

King Heroin is my shepherd, I shall always want,

He maketh me to lie down in the gutters.

He leadeth me beside the troubled waters.

He destroyeth my soul.

With the exception of their use for medical purposes, and therefore under careful control, drugs are destructive. Playing with drugs is foolish, as well as wrong.

3
The Second Step

Art

*I*f it is true that philosophy, the first step in the line of despair, touched only a few people, art, the second step, influenced very many more.

As in philosophy, so in art there is a doorway into the line, and this is provided by the impressionists. When they began they did not see themselves as rebelling against classic concepts. They were interested in a study of light, as was the Englishman Turner who had preceded them. But later their work changed and expressed the new mentality.

Van Gogh and Gauguin
There are three men who stand out above all. They are Van Gogh (a Dutchman), Gauguin and Cézanne (Frenchmen). Each was a genius; they were very real human men, and each produced pictures which show their genius as artists. However, as we enjoy these pictures as art, appreciating their composition, their use of color and all the other things to admire, we must also see their place in the second step in the "line of despair." They are the three pillars of modern art. In each case they tried to find a universal in their art as Leonardo da Vinci[1] had tried many centuries before them. What the philosopher was trying to do within the scope of the whole universe, they now tried to do on

a limited scale on their canvases. As they crossed the threshold of the line of despair, they began a desperate search to find a universal that would give them back reality, something more than just particulars. They were seeking to express a form and a freedom which would be valid in the scope of their discipline, art.

Van Gogh (1853-1890) can be thought of first. Very often people say he committed suicide because he was mentally ill or because Gauguin stole a woman he was interested in. These may have been contributing factors, but the suicide was due to a much more basic problem. There may have been psychological problems, but the final explosion came as a result of disillusionment on a much more fundamental issue. Van Gogh thought to make a new religion in which the sensitive people, the artists, would blaze the trail. For this purpose, he dreamt of starting an artistic community in Arles where he was living. He was joined by Gauguin, but after a few months they began to quarrel violently. Van Gogh's hope of his new religion was gone and soon after, he committed suicide. The death of hope in man had taken place in Van Gogh. He died in despair.

Gauguin (1846-1903) did the same thing. He too was seeking for a universal. He went to Tahiti and there he, following the concepts of Jean-Jacques Rousseau (1712-1778), championed the idea of the noble savage. The savage was to be the return to the primitive, the child of the race, and it was here, going back in time, that he hoped to find the universal. So Gauguin began to paint the beauty of the women he found there. For a time he felt that he had successfully removed himself from the loss of innocence in civilization, and that this was enough. But his last great painting tells the conclusion he came to eventually.

This painting is called *What? Whence? Whither?*[2] and it now hangs in the Boston Museum of Art. The title is painted on a yellow corner on the upper left of the picture, thus making quite sure that anyone who looks at the work will understand its meaning. Elsewhere in discussing the painting, he tells us that we are to look at it the opposite way to normal—namely, from the right to the left.[3] So at the right, where we look first, we see the same kind of beauty as in his other paintings. There is the same exotic symbolism, the same appeal to the sensuous in the concept of the noble savage. But by the time our eye has moved across the canvas to the far left, we see a very different end to the story. He began the painting in 1897 and finished it in 1898. This is what he says about it: "I have finished a philosophical work on this theme, comparable to the gospel. A figure lifts up its arms into the air and, astonished, looks at these two personages who dare to think of their destination." A little farther on he continues:

"Whither? Close to the death of an old woman, a strange, stupid bird concludes: What? The eternal problem that punishes our pride. O Sorrow, thou art my master. Fate, how cruel thou art, and always vanquished, I revolt."[4] When you look at the left-hand side of the picture you see three figures. The first is a young Tahitian woman in all her beauty. Beside her is a poor old woman dying, watched only by a monstrous bird, which has no counterpart in nature. When Gauguin finished this painting, he too tried to commit suicide, though in fact he did not succeed.

Both of these men were attempting to find a humanistic universal. They failed dismally and remained below the line of despair.

Cézanne and Picasso

It was in the basic geometrical form that Cézanne (1839-1906) attempted to discover his universal. Many of his landscape paintings look like taut diaphragms, diaphragms pulled over geometric forms. Later he painted people as geometric forms—for example, *The Bathers*, now hung in the National Gallery in London. As far as we know, tragedy never caught up with him. He died, as far as I have been able to discover, without ever coming to the conclusion of despair.

But someone else carried on from where he left off. This was Picasso (1881-1973). Again we must stress, as we have concerning the others before him, that he was a genius of the first rank, he was overwhelmingly productive, an amazing man as a man, and all of us will find parts of his body of work which will move us, and perhaps will move us deeply.

Picasso saw the work of Cézanne at the large exhibitions of his work in Paris in 1905 and 1907, and discussed the problems involved in Paris in Gertrude Stein's home where many painters used to gather.

Picasso brought together the noble savage of Gauguin, the geometric form of Cézanne and also incorporated something from the African masks that had just become known in Paris, developing between 1906 and 1911 what was to be called Cubism. The great picture of 1906-1907, *Les Demoiselles d'Avignon* (now in the Museum of Modern Art, New York), shows this development. The women on the left are much like those he painted before, but already showing Cézanne's influence in an exaggerated form. In Picasso's private collection which was broken up at his death, there was a small copy of Cézanne's *The Bathers,* made just before Picasso painted *Les Demoiselles d'Avignon.* When one turns to the women on the right, one finds that instead of their being women, they have become demonic beings and symbols as in the African masks. Their humanity has been lost.

Picasso then pushed further. Unlike, say, Renoir, who painted his wife in such a way that she could be recognized (that is, the subject was a particular), Picasso was seeking for a universal. As he abstracted further, one cannot tell whether his women are blondes or brunettes. This is a move towards the universal and away from the particular. But if you go far enough, your abstracted women can become "all women" or even everything. But the difficulty is that when you get to that point the viewer has no clue what he is looking at. You have succeeded in making your own world on your canvas, and in this sense you have become god. But at the same time you have lost contact with the person who views your painting. We have come to the position where we cannot communicate. The problem of modern man's loss of communication and his alienation did not have to wait for the computers and cybernetics. Picasso, the modern man, exhibited this far earlier in his art.

Picasso "solved" his problem with a romantic leap. One day he fell in love, and because he felt the force of love he wrote on the canvases, "*J'aime Eva*" (I love Eva).[5] The painting could have been of anything, a chair or something else abstracted. But suddenly, with the words sprawled across the picture, he was in touch again with the man who looked on. But the communication has no logical relationship to the subject of his canvas. Picasso has failed; his abstraction carried to its logical conclusion has left him with no communication. What remains to him is that which, in his worldview, is a leap.

It is interesting that with the two women he married, Olga and Jacqueline, he painted them at times in the style closer to his earlier pink and blue periods, when as a younger man he was showing his great dexterity in the use of the classical style. But in the ongoing flow of his work, Picasso was the modern man with the brokenness which is involved in it.

This is modern man. This is the concept of truth by which we are surrounded. This is the spirit of the world to which we must say no, no matter what face it puts on, including a theological one. This is what makes the chasm between the last generation and our generation, a break of more than 400 years, a greater break than that between the Renaissance and the generation before ours. The tragedy is not only that these talented men have reached the point of despair, but that so many who look on and admire really do not understand. They are influenced by the concepts, and yet they have never analyzed what it all means.

Mondrian

Mondrian (1872-1944) picked up Picasso's position in art and developed Picasso's style to an extreme conclusion. Mondrian's horizontals and verticals are lovely and magnificent. In architecture they have been used as a practical model. However, for him they were not just horizontals and verticals, for he too was fighting for a universal.

One day I went to the museum in Zurich. They have a big collection of modern paintings there. I went into one of the rooms, and I was aghast. There was a Mondrian with a frame on it. Mondrian did not put frames on his pictures. So I went to the office and asked the man in charge if the Mondrian had a frame on it when he received it. He replied, "No, we put it on." So I said, "Don't you understand? If Mondrian came in here, he would just smash the picture against the wall." As far as I could tell, this was a new idea to him. Really, this man did not seem to understand the picture in his museum, because

Mondrian's whole concept was the building of a universal.

Mondrian painted his pictures and hung them on the wall. They were frameless so that they would not look like holes in the wall. As the pictures conflicted with the room, he had to make a new room. So Mondrian had furniture made for him, particularly by Rietveld, a member of the De Stijl group, and Van der Leck. There was an exhibition in the Stedelijk Museum in Amsterdam in July-September 1951, called "De Stijl," where this could be seen. As you looked, you were led to admire the balance between room and furniture, in just the same way as there is such a good balance in his individual pictures. But if a man came into that room, there would be no place for him. It is a room for abstract balance, but not for man. This is the conclusion modern man has reached, below the line of despair. He has tried to build a system out from himself, but this system has come to the place where there is not room in the universe for man.

Mondrian himself seemed to have come to understand that what he had tried had come to a dead end. He made a big shift in his painting, as shown by the painting *Broadway Boogie Woogie,* which now hangs in the Metropolitan Gallery of Art in New York.

Dada, Marcel Duchamp, the Happenings and the Environments

I have a poem that appeared on page one of the last issue of the magazine called *De Stijl,*[6] which was published by the De Stijl school of painting with which Mondrian was connected. It is written by Hans Arp (1887-1966), one of the members of the original Dada group. This is a translation from the German:

the head downward
the legs upward
he tumbles into the bottomless
from whence he came.
he has no more honour in his body
he bites no more bite of any short meal
he answers no greeting
and is not proud when being adored
the head downward

the legs upward
he tumbles into the bottomless
from whence he came
like a dish covered with hair
like a four-legged sucking chair
like a deaf echotrunk
half full half empty
the head downward
the legs upward
he tumbles into the bottomless
from whence he came.

On the basis of modern man's methodology, whether expressed in philosophy, art, literature or theology, there can be no other ending than this—man tumbling into the bottomless.

Dada is a chance concept. The very word was chosen by chance. One day some people flipped through a French dictionary in Zurich in the Café Voltaire. They put a finger down at random and found it rested on the word *dada*. It means "a rocking horse." And so it was by blind chance that they conceived the name for their school of art.

In the same way they composed their poems. They cut printed words out of the newspaper, threw them in a hat, and picked them out by chance. But these men were deadly serious; it really was no game they were playing.

One such man was Marcel Duchamp (1887-1968), whom every Christian ought to know about. He could be called the high priest of destruction. He is best known by many for his picture *Nude Descending a Stairway*, which is now in the Philadelphia Museum of Art. He was brilliant and destructive—and he meant to destroy. He sought to destroy you from within yourself. The best collection of his work in the world is at the Philadelphia Museum of Art. There is a picture in the Museum of Modern Art in New York, *Le passage de la vierge a la mariee* (the words are written on the canvas and mean, "The passage of the virgin to the married state"). Naturally every man or woman who goes to look at the picture tries to find in the picture something which relates to its title. But no matter how long one looks, one finds no picture of a virgin, nor of a virgin becoming a married woman. Thus he causes the viewer to make himself dirty.

His last work, which no one knew existed, came to light at his death. It is now in the Duchamp collection in the Philadelphia Museum of Art. One must look through a small peephole in an old Spanish door to see it. And it is indeed both pornographic and totally absurd. Why is this placed in the staid Philadelphia Museum of Art by the staid directors? Because it is "Art," and so the message is passed on to the population!

He was the man who, about 1950, gave birth to the *happenings*, and then beyond this the *environments*. The happenings began in New York. We might say that though America was behind at the time of the Armory Show in New York in 1913, today, in modern art and in many other areas under the line of despair, she leads the world.

In the happenings you are put as it were within the picture. You look at people acting; and, as the observer, you are forced to participate. There is always a nonsense element, and there is usually a dirty action as well. Always the observer is involved and is deliberately destroyed.

What are they saying? Everything is chance. Chance, the nothingness, is not just shut up in a framed picture, but it is the entire structure of life. You are in the chance, in the nothingness. You are the destroyed ones.

A good example of the environments was some of the rooms in the art show Art Zero, Art Nul, held in the Stedelijk Museum, Amsterdam, in the summer of 1965. It was the most important show held on the Continent at the time. One entered the rooms in the gallery and looked at objects. But there was something more than mere looking at individual objects; rather you felt permeated by a total context which was almost subliminal. Almost against your wish you got drawn into the mood of the room. I watched young couples going through these rooms in Amsterdam. I knew that most of them did not understand what they saw. But I was certain that by the time they came out, the atmosphere would have had its effect and their moral defenses would have been weakened. They were touched at a deeper level than only the mind, and though the girl could not perhaps analyze what she saw, yet surely she would be more ready to say yes by the time she came out.

In this connection it is important to note that the leaders of the Provos, an anarchist movement in Amsterdam which had been much in the international news through 1966 and 1967, and which has an influence in The Netherlands into the 1980s, said that this movement was the logical result of the exposition program at the Stedelijk Museum in Amsterdam through the previous fifteen years. It is also interesting to note that the Provos called their public demonstrations "Happenings."

These paintings, these poems, and these demonstrations which we have been talking about are the expression of men who are struggling with their appalling lostness. Dare we laugh at such things? Dare we feel superior when we view their tortured expressions in their art? Christians should stop laughing and take such men seriously. Then we shall have the right to speak again to our generation. These men are dying while they live; yet where is our compassion for them? There is nothing more ugly than a Christian orthodoxy without understanding or without compassion.

4
The Third &
Fourth Steps

Music & the General Culture

Just as in philosophy and art, there is a doorway into the line of despair in music as well. Debussy (1862-1918) is the doorway into the field of modern music. It is not as easy to trace the steps in music as it is in visual art; yet the parallels are there. It is not as easy because, inevitably, music has a more subjective element in it. Nevertheless, the general trend from Debussy until now is clear enough.

An exhaustive study, which we cannot undertake here, would involve considering jazz as well as classical music. Such a consideration would involve discussing the shift in form and content in the twenties and thirties when jazz was introduced into the white man's culture, and how the jazz of the forties was the doorway to the despair of a section of modern jazz.[1]

But we will turn our attention to music more in line with the classical tradition. A few illustrations must suffice for the whole. There could be much discussion of detail in this, and yet the total direction of movement is clear. In a later chapter I will deal with the music of John Cage. Here I want to look at *musique concrète.*

Musique Concrète
Musique concrète was developed by Pierre Schaeffer (1910-) in Paris.

Musique concrète is not electronic music—that is, music made electronically and therefore consisting of sounds one does not normally hear. *Musique concrète* is real sound, but seriously distorted. In the beginning it was created by jumping grooves on a phonographic record. Later Pierre Schaeffer invented a machine by which the distortions can be carefully controlled. With his machine he can lift out the source of the sound, split it up, reverse it, slow it down or speed it up—in fact, do just about anything to alter it. To hear the result is to begin to distrust your ears, just as in Op Art you begin to distrust your eyes. The effect is overwhelming. The message which comes across from the distortion is the same as in modern painting. All is relative, nothing is sure, nothing is fixed, all is in flux. *Musique concrète* is just one more way of presenting the uniform message of modern man.

UNESCO has put out a record, entitled *Premiere panorama de musique concrète.*[2] In it is a clear example of what these men are doing, including a selection by one of Schaeffer's friends, Pierre Henry.

He used the human voice speaking Greek. Greek, of course, is exactly the right language to speak in such a setting, for it is the language representative of our Western culture. The voice is first built up out of chance sounds, reflecting modern man's view that man who verbalizes arose by chance in a chance universe with only a future of chance ahead of him. Henry portrays this remorselessly in sound. Suddenly something else begins to happen; the voice begins to degenerate and to fall apart. It is as though one is watching a beautiful woman die and totally decompose before one's eyes. But in this case it is not just the physical body, but the whole person who rots away. It begins to shiver, to shake, to be corrupted. It begins with chance sounds, goes on to the Greek, and ends in chaos. *There can be no other terminus when antithesis dies, when relativism is born and when the possibility of finding any universal which would make sense of the particulars is denied.* This is the consensus of the cultural environment, and this is that world-spirit which we must reject and into which we must speak.

Henry Miller
With this American novelist (1891-1980), we begin our consideration of the fourth step in the line of despair, which I have named general

culture. This could be divided into a number of steps, but I have placed these subjects together under this heading for convenience.

Young people often said that the writing of Henry Miller was not just pornographic but was a philosophical statement. Parents of these young people ask me whether I agree. I reply, "Yes, your child is right. They are certainly dirty books and because of this will soil you. However, they were not intended to be mere pornography. Miller was an antilaw writer. He smashed everything to pieces so that there is nothing left. Even sex is smashed. This is especially devastating because it is often in the sexual area of life that men hope to find some kind of meaning when they have abandoned the search elsewhere."

Not only with Miller but also with other modern writers, we can appreciate the result of this as we notice how they use women in their books. The playmate becomes the plaything, and we are right back with the Marquis de Sade. (I want to talk about the later changed Henry Miller a little farther on.)

Philosophic Homosexuality
Some forms of homosexuality today are of a similar nature, in that they are not just homosexuality but a philosophic expression. One must have understanding for the real homophile's problem. But much modern homosexuality is an expression of the current denial of antithesis. It has led in this case to an obliteration of the distinction between man and woman. So the male and the female as complementary partners are finished. This is a form of homosexuality which is a part of the movement below the line of despair. In much of modern thinking all antithesis and all the order of God's creation is to be fought against—including the male-female distinctions. The pressure toward unisex is largely rooted here. But this is not an isolated problem; it is a part of the world-spirit of the generation which surrounds us. It is imperative that Christians realize the conclusions which are being drawn as a result of the death of absolutes.

John Osborne
In the area of drama, another aspect of general culture, it is important to consider John Osborne (1929-1980), one of the Angry Young Men.

In many ways he is a great playwright, but he has been accurately described as an idealist who has not been able to find an ideal. This is a magnificent description. Osborne is a man of temperament, courage and sensitivity; a man to ride on a charger with his lance at the ready into the great battles of life. He is an idealist by choice, but without an ideal: a man who cares and yet has found nothing worth caring about. His whole approach is summed up with magnificent clarity in his play *Martin Luther*. As history it has weaknesses, but in general it portrays the early part of Luther's life with considerable accuracy. But the moment of truth comes with great force at the very end. Luther is standing with one of his babies in his arms. The elderly head of Luther's old monastery comes to visit him. They face each other. The old man says, "Martin, do you know you are right?" And against all history Osborne makes him reply, "Let's hope so." The lights come on, the curtain is down, and the play is finished. The drama critic of the London *Times* understood. He said, "Isn't it interesting that he had to put in that last line to make it a twentieth-century play!"

Dylan Thomas
When we review modern poetry as part of our own general culture, we find the same tendency to despair. Near the time of his death, Dylan Thomas (1914-1953) wrote a poem called "Elegy."[3] He did not actually put it together himself, so we cannot be too sure of the exact order of the stanzas. But the way it is given below is probably the right order. This poem is by a fellow human being of our generation. He is not an insect on the head of a pin, but shares the same flesh and blood as we do, a man in real despair:

> Too proud to die, broken and blind he died
> The darkest way, and did not turn away,
> A cold kind man brave in his narrow pride
>
> On the darkest day, Oh, forever may
> He lie lightly, at last, on the last, crossed
> Hill, under the grass, in love, and there grow

Young among the long flocks, and never lie lost
Or still all the numberless days of his death, though
Above all he longed for his mother's breast.

Which was rest and dust, and in the kind ground
The darkest justice of death, blind and unblessed.
Let him find no rest but be fathered and found.

I prayed in the crouching room, by his blind bed,
In the muted house, one minute before
Moon, and night, and light. The rivers of the dead

Veined his poor hand I held, and I saw
Through his unseeing eyes to the roots of the sea.
(An old tormented man three-quarters blind),

I am not too proud to cry that He and he
will never never go out of my mind.
All his bones crying, and poor in all but pain.

Being innocent, he dreaded that he died
Hating his God, but what he was was plain:
An old kind man brave in his burning pride.

The sticks of the house were his; his books he owned.
Even as a baby he had never cried;
Nor did he now, save to his secret wound.

Out of his eyes I saw the last light glide.
Here among the light of the lording sky
An old blind man is with me where I go

Walking in the meadow of his son's eye
On whom a world of ills came down like snow.
He cried as he died, fearing at last the spheres

Last sound, the world going out without a breath:
To proud to cry, too frail to check the tears,
And caught between two nights, blindness and death.

O deepest wound of all that he should die
On that darkest day. Oh, he could hide
The tears out of his eyes, too proud to cry.

Until I die he will not leave my side.

In the Festival Hall in London, in one of the higher galleries in the rear corridor, there is a bronze of Dylan Thomas. Anyone who can look at it without compassion is dead. There he faces you with a cigarette at the side of his mouth, the very cigarette hung in despair. It is not good enough to take a man like this or any of the others and smash them as though we have no responsibility for them. This is sensitivity crying out in darkness. But it is not mere emotion; the problem is not on this level at all. These men were not producing art for art's sake, or emotion for emotion's sake. These things are a strong message coming out of their own worldview.

There are many means for killing men, as men, today. They all operate in the same direction: no truth, no morality. You do not have to go to art galleries or listen to the more sophisticated music to be influenced by their message. The common media of cinema and television will do it effectively for you.

Modern Cinema, the Mass Media and the Beatles
We usually divide cinema and television programs into two classes—good and bad. The term *good* as used here means "technically good" and does not refer to morals. The "good" pictures are the serious ones, the artistic ones, the ones with good shots. The "bad" are simply escapist, romantic, only for entertainment. But if we examine them with care, we notice that the "good" pictures are actually the worst pictures. The escapist film may be horrible in its own way, but the so-called "good" pictures have almost all been developed by men

holding the modern philosophy of no certain truth and no certain distinction between right and wrong. This does not imply they have ceased to be men of integrity, but it does mean that the films they produce are tools for teaching their beliefs. Three outstanding modern film producers are Fellini and Antonioni of Italy, and Bergman of Sweden. Of these three producers, Bergman has given the clearest expression perhaps of the contemporary despair. He has said that he deliberately developed the flow of his pictures—that is, the whole body of his movies rather than just individual films—in order to teach existentialism.

His existentialist films led up to but do not include the film *The Silence*. This film was a statement of utter nihilism. Man, in this picture, did not even have the hope of authenticating himself by an act of the will. *The Silence* was a series of snapshots with immoral and pornographic themes. The camera just took them without any comment. "Click, click, click, cut!" That is all there is. Life is like that: unrelated, having no meaning as well as no morals.

In passing, it should be noted that Bergman's presentation in *The Silence* was related to the American "Black Writers" (nihilistic writers), the antistatement novel which was best shown perhaps in Capote's *In Cold Blood*. These, too, were just a series of snapshots without any comment as to meaning or morals.

Such writers and directors have had a large impact upon the mass media, and so the force of the monolithic worldview of our age presses in on every side.

The 1960s was the time of many powerful, philosophic films. The posters advertising Antonioni's *Blow-Up* in the London Underground were inescapable as they told the message of that film: "Murder without guilt; love without meaning." The mass of people may not enter an art museum, may never read a serious book. If you were to explain the drift of modern thought to them, they might not be able to understand it; but this does not mean that they are not influenced by the things they see and hear—including the cinema and what is considered "good," nonescapist television.

No greater illustration could be found of the way these concepts were carried to the masses than "pop" music and especially the work of the Beatles. The Beatles moved through several stages, including the concept of the drug and psychedelic approach. The psychedelic began with their records *Revolver*,[4] "Strawberry Fields Forever" and "Penny Lane."[5] This was developed with great expertness in their record *Sgt. Pepper's Lonely Hearts Club Band*[6] in which psychedelic music, with open statements concerning drug-taking, was knowingly presented as a religious answer. The religious form was the same vague pantheism which predominates much of the new mystical thought today. One indeed does not have to understand in a clear way the modern monolithic thought in order to be infiltrated by it. *Sgt. Pepper's Lonely Hearts Club Band* was an ideal example of the manipulating power of the new forms of "total art." This concept of total art increases the infiltrating power of the message by carefully conforming the technical form used to the message involved. This is used in the theater of the absurd, the Marshall McLuhan type of television program, the new cinema and the new dance with someone like Merce Cunningham. The Beatles used this in *Sgt. Pepper's Lonely Hearts Club Band* by making the whole record one unit so the whole is to be listened to as a unit and makes one thrust, rather than the songs being only something individually. In this record the words, the syntax, the music and the unity of the way the individual songs were arranged form a unity of infiltration.

Those were the days of the ferment of the 1960s. Two things must be said about their results in the 1980s. First, we do not understand the 1980s if we do not understand that our culture went through these *conscious* wrestlings and expressions of the 1960s. Second, most people do not understandably think of all this now, but the results are very much still at work in our culture.

Our culture is largely marked by relativism and ultimate meaninglessness, and when many in the 1980s "join the system" they do so because they have nothing worth fighting for. For most, that was ended by the 1970s. It is significant that when *Sgt. Pepper's Lonely Hearts Club Band* was made a Broadway play (1974, Beacon Theater) it no longer had the ferment; it was "camp" and nostalgia—a museum piece of a bygone time.

5
The Unifying Factor in the Steps of Despair

*T*he line of despair is a unit, and the steps in the line have a distinguishing and unifying mark. With Hegel and Kierkegaard, people gave up the concept of a rational, unified field of knowledge and accepted instead the idea of a leap of faith in those areas which make people distinctive as people—purpose, love, morals and so on. It was this leap of faith that originally produced the line of despair.

The various steps on the line—philosophy, art, music, theater and so on—differ in details, and these details are interesting and important, but in a way they are only incidental. The distinctive mark of the twentieth-century intellectual and cultural climate does not lie in the differences but in the unifying concept. The unifying concept is the concept of a divided field of knowledge.

Whether the symbols to express this are those of painting, poetry or theology is incidental. The vital question is not the symbols used to express these ideas (for example, the words of the existential philosophers or the sounds of *musique concrète*) but the concept of truth and the method of attaining truth. *The watershed is the new way of talking about and arriving at truth, not the terms the individual disciplines use to express these ideas.*

Léopold Sédar Senghor (1906-), president of Senegal, is probably the only real intellectual who is head of a government today anywhere in the world. He studied in France. Senghor has written a book which consists of three political speeches given to groups in his own country. The book is called *On African Socialism*.[1] Some years ago he very kindly sent me an autographed copy of this book. As well as this, he has written some magnificent poetry which has, fortunately, been well translated into English.[2]

As I read his speeches I was very moved. If a man stood up in any of the Western countries and delivered these as political speeches, very few Christians would understand their real significance. The fact that Senghor is an African underlines the need to train our overseas missionaries in a new way, for the problem of communication in our day extends beyond the Sorbonne, Oxford, Cambridge, Harvard or the Massachusetts Institute of Technology to those places which we have traditionally thought of as "the mission-field." The problem of communication does not end at our own shores. Among educated men the new way of thinking is everywhere.

Senghor showed in these speeches on African socialism that he understands the modern issues exceedingly well. He points out that the methodology affecting thought today is the same on both sides of the Iron Curtain. In his book he develops in detail the change from the classical concept of logic (A is not non-A) to the general acceptance today of Hegel's methodology of synthesis.

He points out correctly that originally the Marx and Engels form of communism had an interest in man, which gave it much of its drive. We shall note, of course, that later, as it developed naturally from its presuppositions, man became devalued in the communist state. (The Marx-Engels form of communism should properly be regarded as a Christian heresy. Only Christianity, of all the world's religions, has produced a real interest in man. Buddhism, Hinduism and Islam could never have produced *idealistic* communism because they do not have sufficient interest in the individual.) The one thing about communism which really caught the fancy of idealistic communists was this concern for man. But, as I have said, the source of a real care for people *as individuals* comes from biblical Christianity. Are we losing our impact? It may be due largely to a failure to communicate that we believe that man, in the presence of the God who is there, is truly wonderful. But let us return to Senghor.

He argues that one must not think of Marxism as being primarily an economic theory. Nor must one think that its atheism is central. Atheistic it most certainly is, but that is not the crux of the system. If you want to understand what Marxism really is, says Senghor, you must remember that it rests upon the dialectical methodology.

Senghor goes on to say that he and Senegal cannot accept Marxism's economic theory completely. Neither will they accept its atheism. But they will hold fast to its method of dialectic. In doing this they will follow Teilhard de Chardin.[3] In other words, Senghor realizes that there is no basic difference between the dialectical approach of Marx and that of Teilhard de Chardin.[4] He appreciates that in methodology they are both on the same side. The fact that the Jesuit priest uses the word *god* and Marx does not makes no difference, for the word by itself is meaningless until given content. The really important thing is that they both use the dialectical methodology.

If you want to understand the century you live in, you must realize that it is not the outward form which the dialectic takes which is the real enemy. This may be expressed in theistic or atheistic forms. The real enemy is not the form it takes, but the dialectical methodology itself.

Romanticism Is Dead: Christianity's Opportunity If Antithesis Is Maintained

In one way a Christian ought to be glad that so many live under the line of despair and are fully aware of their position. The Christian should be thankful that when he talks to these people, he does not have to remove page after page of optimistic answers which are against all the evidence and without any base. For Christianity is not romantic; it is realistic.

Christianity is realistic because it says that if there is no truth, there is also no hope; and there can be no truth if there is no adequate base.

It is prepared to face the consequences of being proved false and say with Paul: If you find the body of Christ, the discussion is finished; let us eat and drink, for tomorrow we die.[5] It leaves absolutely no room for a romantic answer. For example, in the realm of morals Christianity does not look over this tired and burdened world and say that it is slightly flawed, a little chipped, but easily mended. Christianity is realistic and says the world is marked with evil and man is truly guilty all along the line. Christianity refuses to say that you can be hopeful for the future if you are basing your hope on evidence of change for the better in mankind. The Christian agrees with the people in genuine despair that the world must be looked at realistically, whether in the area of Being or in morals.

Christianity is poles apart from any form of optimistic humanism. But it also differs from nihilism, for nihilism, though it is correctly realistic, nevertheless can give neither a proper diagnosis nor the proper treatment for its own ills. Christianity has a diagnosis and then a solid foundation for an answer. The difference between Christian realism and nihilism is not that the Christian worldview is romantic. We should be pleased that the romanticism of yesterday has been destroyed. In many ways this makes our task of presenting Christianity to modern man easier than it was for our forefathers.

But to rejoice that romantic answers will no longer do, and to be glad in one sense that men like Dylan Thomas have ended by weeping, does not mean that we should not be filled with compassion for our fellowmen. To live below the line of despair is not to live in paradise, whether that of a fool or any other kind. It is in a real sense to have a foretaste of hell now, as well as the reality in the life to come. Many of our most sensitive people have been left absolutely naked by the destruction. Should we not grieve and cry before God for such people?

In this situation which so desperately cries out for the remedy which only biblical Christianity can give, we seem to be failing. This cannot be due to lack of opportunity; already men are partway to the gospel, for they too believe that man is *dead,* dead in the sense of being meaningless. Christianity alone gives the reason for this meaningless-ness, that their revolt has separated them from God who exists, and thus gives them the true explanation of the position to which they have come. But we cannot take advantage of our opportunity, *if we let go* in either thought or practice the methodology of antithesis (that is, that A is A and A is not non-A). If a thing is true, the opposite is not true; if a thing is right, the opposite is wrong.

If our own young people within the churches and those of the world outside see us playing with the methodology of synthesis, in our teaching and evangelism, in our policies and institutions, we can never expect to take advantage of this unique moment of opportunity presented by the death of romanticism. If we let go of our sense of antithesis, we will have nothing left to say.

Moreover, not only will we have nothing to say, we become nothing. Christianity ceases to exist, though it may still keep its outward institutional form. Christianity demands antithesis, not as some abstract concept of truth but in the fact that God exists, and in personal justification. The biblical concept of justification is a total, personal antithesis. Before justification, we were dead in the kingdom of darkness. The Bible says that in the moment that we accept Christ we pass from death to life. This is total antithesis at the level of the individual man. Once we begin to slip over into the other methodology—a failure to hold on to an absolute which can be known by the whole man, including what is logical and rational in him—historic Christianity is destroyed, even if it seems to keep going for a time. We may not know it, but when this occurs the marks of death are upon it, and it will soon be one more museum piece.

To the extent that anyone gives up the mentality of antithesis, he has moved over to the other side, even if he still tries to defend orthodoxy or evangelicalism. If Christians are to take advantage of the death of romanticism, we must consciously build back the mentality and practice of antithesis among Christians in doctrine and life. We must do it by our teaching and by example in our attitude toward compromise, both ecclesiastically and in evangelism. To fail to exhibit that we take truth seriously at those points where there is a cost in our doing so is to push the next generation into the relative, dialectical millstream that surrounds us.

Finally, and with due reverence, may I emphasize that not only should we have genuine compassion for the lost among whom we live, but also concern for our God. We are his people, and if we get caught up in the other methodology, we have really blasphemed, discredited and dishonored him—for the greatest antithesis of all is that God exists as opposed to his not existing; he is the God who is there.

Section Two

The Relationship
of the New Theology
to the
Intellectual Climate

1
The Fifth Step

Theology

Departure from Biblical Christianity
Modern existential theology finds its origin in Kierkegaard, as does secular existentialism. They are related together at the very heart of their systems—that is, "the leap of faith." Theology comes as the last step, but it is by no means isolated from the rest of the cultural consensus we have been reviewing.

There is diversity within the unity of the new theology. There is a difference, for example, between neo-orthodoxy and the new liberalism following the new Heidegger. Careful scholarship demands that we appreciate such differences. But if we miss the unity which binds together all expressions of modern theology, we have missed the essential point.

At the time of the Reformation, the reformers were confronted with a total system. They did not say that there were no Christians within the Roman Catholic Church, nor did they say that there were no differences in the teaching and emphases of the various Roman Catholic Orders. But they understood that there was one underlying system which bound every part of the Church together, and it was this system *as a system* that they said was wrong and in opposition to the teaching of the Bible.

Today evangelicals are again confronted with an overwhelming consensus, a methodology accepted by theologians on every side. Thus, while one can get some insights (for example, Bultmann has some good exegesis in some details), yet this is not the place for ambivalent judgment—nor mere disagreement concerning details—we must realize that their system *as a system* is wrong.

As Senghor pointed out that the basic factor of Marxism was neither its economic theory nor its atheism but its dialectical methodology, so the unifying factor of the new theology is its wrong methodology. Since its concept of truth is wrong, what sounds right often means something entirely different from that which historic Christianity means by the same phrase. It is naive to discuss the theological questions as theological questions until one has considered what truth means to the one who is making the theological statements.

Theology has been through the same process as philosophy, though several decades later. Prior to Hegel, rationalistic man was still trying to draw his circles to encompass the whole of life. Then came the line of despair. Naturalistic theology has followed this very closely. The old liberal theologians in Germany began by accepting the presupposition of the uniformity of natural causes as a closed system. Thus they rejected everything miraculous and supernatural, including the supernatural in the life of Jesus Christ. Having done that, they still hoped to find a historical Jesus in a rational, objective, scholarly way by separating the supernatural aspect of Jesus' life from the "true history."

But they failed in the same way that the rationalistic philosophers had failed. They too were caught in the round room without an exit. Their search for the historical Jesus was doomed to failure. The supernatural was so intertwined with the rest that if they ripped out all the supernatural, there was no Jesus left! If they removed all the supernatural, no historical Jesus remained; if they kept the historical Jesus, the supernatural remained as well.

After their failure they could have done two things in order to continue in a rational and logical framework. They could have left their rationalism and returned to the biblical theology of the Reformation (which they had rejected on the basis of naturalistic presuppositions); or they could have become nihilistic concerning thought and life. But instead of choosing either of these two rational alternatives, they chose a third way, just as the philosophers had already done—a way which had been unthinkable to educated man before this, and which involved the division of the concept of truth.

Why did theology follow philosophy in this tremendously important step? For two reasons: first, their old optimistic rationalism had failed to produce a historically credible Jesus, once the miraculous had been rejected; second, since the surrounding consensus of thought which they were carefully following was normative to them, when philosophy developed in this direction, they eventually followed.

So it was not so much neo-orthodoxy which destroyed the older form of liberalism, even though Karl Barth's teaching might have been the final earthquake which shook down the tottering edifice; rather, it had already been destroyed from within. To say it in another way—if Barth had spoken fifty years before, it is doubtful if any would have listened.

Neo-orthodoxy gave no new answer. What existential philosophy had already said in secular language was now expressed in theological language. We can represent it like this:

THE NONRATIONAL AND NONLOGICAL	A crisis first-order experience. Faith as an optimistic leap without verification or communicable content.
THE RATIONAL AND LOGICAL	The Scripture full of mistakes—pessimism.

Neo-orthodoxy leaped to what I call the "upper story" in order to try to find something which would give hope and meaning to life. The "lower story" is the position to which their presuppositions would have rationally and logically brought them.

So theology too has gone below the line of despair:

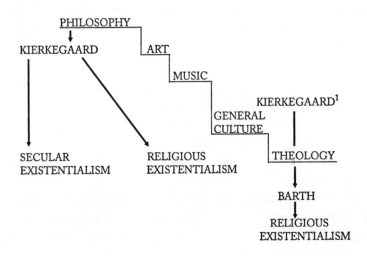

The new theology has given up hope of finding a unified field of knowledge. Hence, in contrast to biblical and Reformation theology, it is antitheology.

Seen in this way it is naive to study the new theology as if it were a subject on its own. Some years ago I was speaking at one of the most solidly biblical seminaries in the world. I began by saying that if our American theologians had understood the Armory Show of 1913 in New York, when modern art was first shown in the United States, perhaps the big denominations in American would not have been captured by the liberals in the thirties. By that time the trends which would come much later in theology were being foreshadowed in art. This is why, earlier in this book, I gave 1913 as such an important date. Had the Christians understood the message of this art at the Armory Show, it would have been a tremendous opportunity to have been ahead rather than to have lagged behind. Conservative theology has not yet caught up. It has been far too provincial, isolated from general cultural thinking.

Karl Barth was the doorway in theology into the line of despair. He continued to hold to the day of his death the higher (negative) critical theories which the liberals held and yet, by a leap, sought to bypass the two rational alternatives—a return to the historic view of Scripture or an acceptance of pessimism. After the first edition of his *Commentary on the Epistle to the Romans,* he no longer acknowledged his debt to Kierkegaard. However, still believing the higher critical theories, his "leap" continued to be the base of his optimistic answers. In later years, as his followers have carried his views forward, he drew back from their consistent extensions. But as Kierkegaard, with his leap, opened the door to existentialism in general, so Karl Barth opened the door to the existentialistic leap in theology. As in other disciplines the basic issue is the shift in epistemology.

He has been followed by many more, men like Reinhold Niebuhr and Paul Tillich. They may differ in details, but their struggle is the same—it is the struggle of modern man who has given up a unified field of knowledge. As far as the theologians are concerned, they have separated religious truth from contact with science on the one hand and history on the other. Their new system is not open to verification; it must simply be believed.

Thus, though their position rests on a "liberal" view of Scripture, yet in the new theology the real issue is now not only their view of Scripture but their divided view of truth.

2
Modern Mysticism

Despair Beyond Despair

*T*he despair of modern man takes many forms. It is despair in depth in that it tends to use formulations and forms which seem to give hope and yet in the nature of the case lead to more profound depths of despair.

Modern nihilism is the simplest form of despair. For example, it is transparently clear in Gauguin's painting *What? Whence? Whither?* and in *musique concrète*. Nihilism accepts the conclusion that everything is meaningless and chaotic.

The second level of despair is the acceptance of the dichotomy we have been talking about:

A blind optimistic hope of meaning, based on a nonrational leap of faith

---

The rational and the logical which gives no meaning

To feel the force of this deeper form of despair, we must keep in mind that the "upstairs" and the "downstairs" of this dichotomy are in two totally watertight compartments. There is *no* interchange between them. *The downstairs has no relationship to meaning; the upstairs no relationship to reason.* Rationalistic man, having given up the methodology of antithesis (if a thing is true, the opposite is not true), has been forced to a nonunified concept of knowledge and consequently to a resultant monstrous total antithesis between rationality and meaning. In the rational downstairs, man is only a machine. In the nonrational upstairs, he is less than a Greek "shade." The films *Last Year in Marienbad, Juliet of the Spirits,* and *Blow-Up* put this latter point with force, showing man as he is upstairs without categories.

The dichotomy was presented as an answer to the despair of simple nihilism; but this dichotomy is really a more profound form of despair. It means that man has both divided any unified concept of knowing and also—and this is worse—divided the unity of himself, because rationality is a part of every man. The individual man cannot even communicate to himself in his own thinking except on the basis of antithesis. So he thinks, "I love her," or "The blossom on that tree is beautiful," but these are a quite meaningless jumble of words unless they stand in antithesis to the possibilities that he dislikes her or that the blossom is ugly. This means in practice that a man cannot totally reject the methodology of antithesis, however much his system leads him to it, unless he experiences the total alienation from himself brought about by some form of mental breakdown.

Therefore, those who have sponsored the modern dichotomy of reason and meaning have not been able to live with it. Jean-Paul Sartre quarreled with Camus because he felt Camus was not being consistent to their basic presuppositions. This was true, but then neither was Sartre consistent when he signed the Algerian Manifesto. When he did this, it was not simply in order to authenticate his being by a neutral act of the will (as in the illustration of the old lady we gave concerning Sartre in chapter two of section one), because then it would have made no difference if he had done the opposite. Rather, it was because he took up a deliberately moral attitude and said it was an unjust and dirty war. His left-wing political position which he took as a moral issue is another illustration of the same inconsistency.

As far as many secular existentialists have been concerned, from the moment Sartre signed the Algerian Manifesto he was regarded as an apostate from his own position and toppled from his place of leadership of the avant-garde.

What was true of Camus and Sartre—that they could not live with the conclusions of their system—has been true for men on every step of the line of despair, whether in philosophy, art, music or literature. The result of not being able to stand in the honest integrity of their despair on either level (that of nihilism or that of a total dichotomy between reason and meaninglessness) has led to modern thought being shifted yet one stage further into a *third* level of despair, a level of mysticism with nothing there.

Theology and Semantic Mysticism

Neo-orthodoxy at first glance seems to have an advantage over secular existentialism. It appears to have more substance in its optimistic expressions than its secular counterpart. As we have seen, one difficulty of the final experience is that no one has found a way to communicate this experience—not even to himself. But in the new theology, use is made of certain religious words which have a connotation of personality and meaning to those who hear them. Real communication is not in fact established, but an *illusion* of communication is given by employing words rich in connotations. Expressing the inexpressible existential experience in religious connotation words gives an illusion of communication.

Carl Gustav Jung (1875-1961) speaks of the collective unconscious which emerges from the race as a whole. I think he is mistaken in his thinking, especially in the evolutionary origin which he gives it. And yet there is a certain memory in a culture that is carried on in *its language*. Such a language-related memory, I suggest, is a better explanation for what Jung calls the collective unconscious.[1]

The Use of Words and Symbols

Every word has two parts. There is the dictionary definition, and there is the connotation. Words may be synonymous by definition, but have completely different connotations. Therefore we find that when such a symbol as *the cross* is used, whether in writing or painting, a certain connotation stirs the mind of people brought up in a Christian culture, even if they have rejected Christianity. (Of course, the use of words in this way does not only apply to the symbols of Christianity, but to those of other religions as well.) So when the new theology uses such words, without definition, an illusion of meaning is given which is pragmatically useful in arousing deep motivations.

This is something beyond emotion. An *illusion of communication and content* is given so that when a word is used in this deliberately undefined way, the hearer "thinks" he knows what it means. The use of the word *pantheism* is a good example. Though it really speaks of something absolutely and finally impersonal, yet the *theism* part of the word causes a reaction of acceptance, since *theism* carries overtones of personality. Now suppose you were to substitute the word *pan-every-thingism* (which is what it really means). The whole reaction would be different.

It is also important to notice that the new theology has tried to draw on the prestige surrounding the use of the word *symbol* in the scientific world, but with a totally changed concept of symbol. In science the use of symbol is valuable in that it is *well-defined*, at least for two people, the person who uses it and at least one other. It is said that when Einstein first propounded his theory of relativity, perhaps only three or four men in the world understood it at first sight. But he would never have written it in the form he did if at least these three or four had not been able to understand it as a well-defined communication of content. So the scientific symbol has become an important tool for writing increasingly lengthy formulae with greater accuracy. In other words, it has value according to the sharpness of its definition.

But the new theology uses the concept of symbol in exactly the opposite way. The only thing the theological and scientific uses have in common is the *word* symbol. *To the new theology, the usefulness of a symbol is in direct proportion to its obscurity.* There is connotation, as in the word *god*, but there is no definition. The secret of the strength of neo-orthodoxy is that these religious symbols with a connotation of personality give an illusion of meaning, and as a consequence it appears to be more optimistic than secular existentialism. One could not find a clearer example of this than Tillich's phrase "God behind God."

At first acquaintance this concept gives the feeling of spirituality. "I do not ask for answers, I just believe." This sounds spiritual, and it deceives many fine people. These are often young men and women who are not content only to repeat the phrases of the intellectual or spiritual *status quo*. They have become rightly dissatisfied with a dull, dusty, introverted orthodoxy given only to pounding out the well-known clichés. The new theology sounds spiritual and vibrant, and they are trapped. But the price they pay for what seems to be spiritual is high, for to operate in the upper story using undefined religious terms is to fail to know and function on the level of the whole man. The answer is not to ask these people to return to the poorness of the *status quo*, but to a living orthodoxy which is concerned with the whole man, including the rational and the intellectual, in his relationship to God.

Whenever men say they are looking for greater reality, we must show them at once the reality of *true* Christianity. This is real because it is concerned with the God who is there and who has spoken to us about himself, not just the use of the symbol *god* or *christ* which sounds spiritual but is not. The men who merely use the symbol ought to be pessimists, for the mere *word* god or the *idea* god is not a sufficient base for the optimism they display.

Speaking rationally, the new theologians are in the same position as Pierre Schaeffer with his *musique concrète*. But it is as though they were asking us by a leap of faith to hear *musique concrète* as if it were the same as the unity and diversity of J. S. Bach. This is the kind of "believism" which is demanded by this theology. *The optimistic jump is a necessity because man is still created in the image of God, whatever he may say about himself, and as such he cannot go on living in meaninglessness.* The jump of the new theology is upon the basis of religious and therefore personal terms which give the connotation of personality, meaning and communication. It is no more than a jump into an undefinable, irrational, semantic mysticism.

Even here the new theology is not unique. There are many secular parallels for this use of the stratagem of connotation words to try to alleviate the despair caused by the loss of a rational meaning and purpose. We will now look at some examples in the different disciplines.

The Origins of Semantic Mysticism—Leonardo da Vinci

The best way to understand how modern man has been forced, often against his natural inclination, into these various levels of despair, which he has tried to alleviate by the use of loaded connotation words in the upper story, is by looking at one of the most brilliant men of the Renaissance, Leonardo da Vinci (1452-1519).

Leonardo died as the Reformation was beginning. Francis I, king of France, who took him to France where he died, was the king to whom John Calvin addressed his *Institutes*. As a Renaissance humanist, Leonardo gave an answer to life which was a complete contrast to what the reformers were giving.

The Reformation gave rise to a definite culture, particularly in Northern Europe, and the humanistic elements of the Renaissance (of which Leonardo was a spokesman) ultimately gave rise to the despair of modern man which is now destroying that culture. Listen to what Giovanni Gentile, known, until his death, as Italy's greatest modern philosopher, has to say about Leonardo:

> The unity of the inward illuminates the fantasy; and the intellect comes to break up this unity into the endless multiplicity of sensible appearances. Hence the anguish and the innermost tragedy of this universal man, divided between his irreconcilable worlds, leaves in the mind an infinite longing, made up as it were of regret and sadness. It is the longing for a Leonardo different from the Leonardo that he was, one who could have gathered himself up at each phase and remained, closed himself off either altogether in his fantasy or altogether in his intelligence.[2]

What Gentile is saying is this—that Leonardo as the first real mathematician in the modern sense really understood the problem with which modern man is now grappling. He understood that if man starts with himself alone and logically and rationally moves through mathematics, he never comes to a universal, only to particulars and mechanics. The problem can be formulated thus: how can finite man produce a unity which will cover these particulars? And if he cannot, how can these particulars have unity and meaning for him?

Leonardo was a Neo-Platonist who followed Ficino, and he tried to resolve the dilemma on his canvas by painting the soul. The use of the word *soul* here does not mean the Christian idea of soul, but the universal. Thus, for example, he thought he could, as a painter, sketch the universal baby which would cover the particulars for all babies. But he never achieved it, any more than Picasso did in painting his abstractions. But there is a strong difference between these two. Leonardo was not a modern man and therefore could not accept modern man's irrational solution. So Leonardo died in despondency, for he would never let go of his hope of finding a unified field of knowledge which included both the universal and the particular, both mathematics and meaning. Had he been willing to accept an irrational dichotomy, as those who have extended the thinking of Kierkegaard have, he could have been at ease. But for him this would have been an impossible answer; men of his day, humanists though they may have been, would never have accepted such an irrational solution.

So there is an unbroken line from the humanism of the Renaissance to the modern philosophy, but in the process modern man accepted the "leap" which philosophers of the past would never have accepted, and have moved into three areas of despair: (1) simple nihilism; (2) the acceptance of the absolute dichotomy; (3) a semantic mysticism based on connotation words.

This new mysticism does not expect to find a unified field of knowledge. It has firmly concluded that the awful contradictory situation whereby meaning and true rationality (the upper and lower story) are irrevocably separated is intrinsic to the nature of the universe. On the other hand, the old romanticism never gave up the search to find a rational unity between the upper and lower story. This is the fundamental difference between them.

Nature and Grace
This difference exists between the new mysticism and the old formu-

lation of nature and grace.

After Thomas Aquinas (1227-1274), men spent much time in seeking the relationship and possible unity of nature and grace. Before him, the emphasis of the Byzantine thinkers was all on heavenly things, while after him, as a result of Aquinas's emphasis on Aristotle, nature also became important. This was given expression in the painting of Cimabue (1240-1302) and Giotto (1267-1337) and in the poetry of Dante (1265-1321), Boccaccio (1313-1375) and Petrarch (1304-1374). By the time the full Renaissance had flooded Europe, nature had all but overwhelmed grace. We can represent their thought in this way:

GRACE, the higher:	God the Creator; heaven and heavenly things, the unseen and its influence on the earth; man's soul; unity.
NATURE, the lower:	The created; earth and earthly things; the visible and what it (nature + man) does on earth; man's body; diversity.

At first glance this might seem to be the same as the modern dichotomy:

THE NONRATIONAL AND NONLOGICAL

THE RATIONAL AND LOGICAL

But the difference between these two concepts is so fundamental as to be qualitative rather than quantitative.

The struggle concerning *nature and grace* was the struggle to find a meaning for these together, and philosophers always hoped for a unity between the two on the basis of reason. (In passing, one must add that this question of nature and grace can only be solved by the full biblical system, and it was because these men tried to find a rationalistic or humanistic answer that they failed.) But modern man has given up all hope of finding a unified answer to the question of nature and grace. Therefore he describes it differently, and the difference in his formulation indicates his despair.[3] Modern man now formulates it like this:

Contentless faith (no rationality)

Rationality (no meaning)

To understand this at a profound level is to comprehend how completely modern man's despair *is* despair. All the new theology and mysticism is nothing more than a faith contrary to rationality, deprived of content and incapable of contentful communication. You can bear "witness" to it, but you cannot discuss it. Rationality and faith are out of contact with each other.

Let us now change the horizontal line a bit and see it as a line of *anthropology*. Below this line is the area of man. All that the new theology has above this line is the "philosophic other," a metaphysical infinite, which is unknown and unknowable. Like this:

god equals the Philosophic Other, unknown and unknowable

---

the word *god* undefined

The new theology is totally below the line of anthropology. It knows nothing of man being created in the image of God, nor of God revealing himself truly in the Scriptures.

The important thing to note is that while for them nothing can be known above the line, yet nevertheless they go on using the word "god."

Probably the best way to describe this concept of modern theology is to say that it is faith in faith, rather than faith directed to an object which is actually there. Some years ago at a number of universities I spoke on the topic "Faith v. Faith," speaking on the contrast between Christian faith and modern faith. The same word, *faith*, is used, but has an opposite meaning. Modern man cannot talk about the object of his faith, only about the faith itself. So he can discuss the existence of his faith and its "size" as it exists against all reason, but that is all. Modern man's faith turns inward.

In Christianity the value of faith depends upon the object towards which the faith is directed. So it looks outward to the God who is there, and to the Christ who in history died upon the cross once for all, finished the work of atonement, and on the third day rose again in space and in time. This makes Christian faith open to discussion and verification. On the other hand, the new theology is in a position where faith is introverted because it has no certain object, and where the preaching of the *kerygma* is infallible since it is not open to rational discussion. This position, I would suggest, is actually a greater despair and darkness than the position of those modern men who commit suicide.

3
Modern Mysticism in Action

Art & Language

The Tension of Being Man

There is a real tension in being a modern man because no one can live at ease in the area of despair. A Christian knows that this is because man has been made in the image of God and though man is fallen, separated from God by his true guilt, yet nevertheless he has not become a machine. The fallenness of man does not lead to *machineness*, but to *fallen-manness*. Therefore, when people feel this utter despair, there is a titanic pressure, like being extruded (against all the long history of reasoned thinking) to accept a dichotomy, and then later to accept some mysticism which gives an illusion of unity to the whole.

I remember sitting in a Lyons' Corner House near Marble Arch in London some years ago, talking to a brilliant young physicist. I asked him about the latest work he was doing, and he told me about a new idea that he thought might solve Einstein's problem concerning electromagnetism and gravity. He became very enthusiastic about this, because I knew enough about the subject to stimulate him, and he was far away in his thought. Then I brought him back by saying, "This is fine for the Christian, who really knows who he is, to say that the material universe may finally be reduced to energy particles moving in opposite directions in a vortex, but what about your naturalistic colleagues? What happens to them when they go home to their wives and families at night?"

He paused for a moment and then said, "Oh, Dr. Schaeffer, they just have to live in a dichotomy."

The very "mannishness" of man refuses to live in the logic of the position to which his humanism and rationalism have brought him. To say that I am only a machine is one thing; to live consistently as if this were true is quite another.

Again I remember one night crossing the Mediterranean on the way from Lisbon to Genoa. It was a beautiful night. On board the boat I encountered a young man who was building radio stations in North Africa and Europe for a big American company. He was an atheist, and when he found out I was a pastor, he anticipated an evening's entertainment, so he started in. But it did not go quite that way. Our conversation showed me that he understood the implications of his position and tried to be consistent concerning them. After about an hour I saw that he wanted to draw the discussion to a close, so I made one last point which I hoped he would never forget, not because I hated him, but because I cared for him as a fellow human being. He was accompanied by his lovely little Jewish wife. She was very beautiful and full of life, and it was easy to see, by the attention he paid her, that he really loved her.

Just as they were about to go to their cabin, in the romantic setting of the boat sailing across the Mediterranean and a beautiful full moon shining outside, I finally said to him, "When you take your wife into your arms at night, can you be sure she is there?"

I hated to do it to him, but I did it knowing that he was a man who would really understand the implications of the question and not forget. His eyes turned, like a fox caught in a trap, and he shouted at me, "No, I am not always sure she is there," and walked into his cabin. I am sure I spoiled his last night on the Mediterranean, and I was sorry to do so. But I pray that as long as he lives he will never forget that when his system was placed against biblical Christianity, it could not stand, not on some abstract point, but at the central point of *his own humanity*, in the reality of love.

In a different but related way this is also true of a man like Bernard Berenson (1865-1959). He was the world's greatest expert on Renaissance art during his lifetime. He graduated from Harvard and lived most of his later life in Florence. He was such an authority on his subject that when he dated and priced a picture, it was generally accepted as decisive. He was a truly "modern" man and accepted sexual amorality. Therefore when he took Mary Costelloe (sister of the American essayist Logan Pearsall Smith) away from her husband, he lived with her for a number of years until her husband died and then married her (the Costelloes' marriage was Roman Catholic, and so a divorce could not be arranged). When Berenson eventually married her, they had an agreement that they would both be free to engage in extramarital affairs, and both took advantage of the agreement many times. They lived this way for forty-five years. When anyone chided Berenson, he would simply say, "You are forgetting the animal basis of our nature." Thus he was perfectly willing in his private life to accept a completely animal situation.

But in contrast to this, he expressed a completely different view where his real love and true integration point—Renaissance art—was concerned. "Bernard Berenson found that modern figure painting in general was not based on seeing, on observing, but on exasperation and on the preconceived assumption that the squalid, the sordid, the violent, the bestial, the misshapen, in short . . . low life was the only reality!"[1] In the area of sexual morals he was perfectly willing to live consistently to his view of life as an animal. But in the area which had become his attempt to find an integration point, that of art, he was prepared to say that he disliked modern art *because it is bestial!* No man like Berenson can live with his system. Every truly modern man is forced to accept some sort of leap in theory or practice, because the pressure of his own humanity demands it. He can say what he will concerning what he himself is; but no matter what he says he is, he still is man.

These kinds of leaps, produced in desperation as an act of blind faith, are totally different from the faith of historic Christianity. On the basis of biblical Christianity a rational discussion and consideration can take place, because it is fixed in the stuff of history. When Paul was asked whether Jesus was raised from the dead, he gave a completely nonreligious answer, in the twentieth-century sense. He said: "There are almost 500 living witnesses; go and ask them!"[2] This is the faith that involves the whole man, including his reason; it does not ask for a belief into the void. As the twentieth-century mentality would understand the concept of religion, the Bible is a nonreligious book.

Mysticism in Art—Paul Klee and Salvador Dali
In one of his writings Paul Klee (1879-1940) speaks of some of his paintings as though they were a kind of artistic Ouija board. (A Ouija board is a little board used by spiritists upon which participants place their hands and then ask questions. The spirits are supposed to move the board and spell out the answers.)

Paul Klee and men like him use art like a Ouija board not because they believe there are any spirits there to speak, but because they hope that the universe will push through and cause a kind of automatic writing, this time in painting. It is an automatic writing with no one there, as far as anyone knows, but the hope is that the "universe" will speak.

Klee not only painted and drew, but also wrote about his work to explain what he was doing. In his essay "Creative Confession"[3] he has this to say: "People used to reproduce things seen on earth—things which had been or would be seen with pleasure. Today the reality of visible objects has been revealed and the belief has been expressed that, in relation to the universe, the visible is only an isolated case and that other truths exist latently and are in the majority." He goes on to employ a phrase, *plastic polyphony,* which means "elements and their regrouping." To Klee the word *elements* is a technical term. He defined this term in his essay as "points, the energy of the line, surface and space." He is referring to these as he continues: "But that [the elements] is not art in its most exalted form. In its most exalted form there is behind the ambiguity a last mystery and at that point the light of the intellect dies away miserably." So he too allows himself to be placed in the dichotomy. He hopes that somehow art will find a meaning, not because there is a spirit there to guide the hand, but because through it the universe will speak even though it is impersonal in its basic structure.

I would add that in almost all forms of the new mysticism there is a growing acceptance of the ideas of pantheism. The West and the East are coming together, and these pantheistic concepts are one of the strongest elements in the semantic mysticism of which we are speaking.

In his earlier days Salvador Dali (1901-1989) was a surrealist. As such he united the teaching of Dada with the concept of the Freudian unconscious, because this is what surrealism is. But at a certain point he could stand this no longer, and so he changed.

One day he painted his wife and called the picture *The Basket of Bread*. It is obvious from looking at the picture that on that day he really loved her. It is the same kind of situation as when Picasso wrote on his canvas, "I love Eva." Before I had heard of any change in Dali, I saw a reproduction of this picture, and it was obvious that there was something different being produced. It is significant that his wife has kept this painting in her private collection.[4]

So on this particular day Dali gave up his surrealism and began his new series of mystical paintings. He had, in fact, already painted two other pictures with the title *A Basket of Bread*, one in 1926 and one in 1945. These just showed baskets of coarse Spanish bread. But this third picture, also painted in 1945, was of his wife Galarina, and shows her with one breast exposed. Her name is written on the picture, and the wedding ring is prominent on her finger.

The second painting in his new style was called *Christ of Saint John of the Cross*, painted in 1951, which now hangs in the Glasgow Art Gallery. Salvador Dali has written about this painting in a little folder on sale in the museum: "In artistic texture and technique I painted the *Christ of Saint John of the Cross* in the manner in which I had already painted my *Basket of Bread*, which even then, more or less unconsciously, represented the Eucharist to me."

What does he mean? He means that when he looks at his wife one day, really loving her, and paints her with one breast exposed, this is equated by him to the Eucharist—not in the sense that anything really happens, either in the Roman Catholic Mass, or that anything really happened back there in Palestine 2,000 years ago, but his love jarred him into a modern type of mysticism.[5]

In this painting he differed from Picasso's *J'aime Eva*. As far as we know, Picasso never really went beyond the problems of his individual loves; but to Dali it became the key to a mysticism. In order to express the leap that he felt forced to take, he picked up Christian symbols, not to express Christian concepts but a nonrational mysticism.

After these two paintings he painted his next Crucifixion, called *Corpus Hyperoubus*, now in the Metropolitan Museum of Art in New York, and then later *The Sacrament of the Last Supper*, which is in the National Gallery of Art in Washington. This latter painting expresses his thought vividly. As the viewer looks at Jesus, he can see the background showing through him; he is a mist. This is no Christ of history. Above him stands a great human figure with arms outspread, its head cut off by the top edge of the picture. No one is sure what this figure is. However, it is strongly reminiscent of the "Yakso" which in Hindu art and architecture often stands behind the "saviors" ("savior" here bearing no relation to the Christian idea). Yaksa and Yaksi connect vegetable life with man on one side and the complete concept of pantheism on the other. I *think* this is what Dali is also saying by this cut-off figure in the painting. Whether this is so or not, the symbolism of the form of the "room" is clear because it is constructed by means of the ancient Greek symbol of the universe.

In an interview Dali connects this religious interest of his later life with science's reduction of matter to energy: ". . . the discoveries in quantum physics of the nature of energy, that matter becomes energy, a state of dematerialization. I realized that science is moving toward a spiritual state. It is absolutely astonishing, the mystical approach of the most eminent scientists: the declaration of Max Planck and the views of Pierre Teilhard de Chardin, a great Jesuit scientist: that man in his constant evolution is coming closer and closer to a oneness with God."

Here he relates his own mysticism and the religious mysticism of Teilhard de Chardin to impersonal dematerialization rather than to anything personal. He is quite correct and need not have confined himself to modern liberal Roman Catholicism but could also have included the Protestant forms of the new theology as well.

It is perfectly possible to pick up nondefined Christian symbols or words and use them in this new mysticism, while giving them opposite meanings. Their use does not necessarily imply that they have Christian meanings. Dali's secular mysticism, like the new theology, gives the philosophic other or impersonal "everything" a personal name in order to get relief by connotation from meaninglessness.

Mysticism in Language—Martin Heidegger

Because he could not live with his existentialism, Heidegger as an older man moved his position. His new position rests on these points: (1) something, *Being*, is there; (2) this something makes itself known; (3) language is one with Being and makes Being known. We can never know rationally about what is there (brute fact), but language does reveal that something is there. Thus language is already itself an interpretation (a hermeneutic).

He postulates that there was long ago an era, before Aristotle (and before the entrance of rationality), when men spoke in Greek in such a way that the universe was speaking ideally. He then tries to transfer this to all of man's language—not the content of what is spoken but simply the existence of language. In this way the existence of language becomes for Heidegger the mysticism by which he tries to find relief from his previous existential dichotomy. It is semantic mysticism because it does not deal with content in language but simply language as such. Man speaking becomes the mouthpiece of the impersonal "What is" (Being). The impersonal and unknown Being speaks through the being who speaks (verbalizes)—that is, man.

This could be a quite correct view if there were any personality behind man to speak meaningfully to and through man. But because Heidegger is a rationalist and begins absolutely from himself, he cannot accept that a person behind man has spoken. So he is shut up to his particular form of semantic mysticism. The word *language* is a connotation word which seems to involve personality. The whole solution hangs on the connotation inherent in the one word *language*.

At the end of his book *What Is Philosophy?*[6] he says that in our modern day this use of language is found particularly in the poet. So the conclusion of this view is that we are to listen to the poet. This does not mean we are to listen to the *content* of what the poet says, but to listen to the fact that *there is a speaking which exists.* That is all.

There is a strong parallel between Klee and Heidegger here. Both speak of their hope that somehow the universe will speak either through art or language. However, Heidegger has much more importance in the flow of modern thought because by using connotation words he has become the father of a new form of the new theology—the new liberalism. There is no real difference between Heidegger's secular mysticism and the mysticism of the new theology.

4
Modern Mysticism in Action

Music & Literature

Mysticism in Music—Leonard Bernstein and John Cage
Leonard Bernstein's Third Symphony, which he has recorded with the New York Philharmonic Orchestra, gives an example of the same kind of mysticism in music. It is called the *Kaddish Symphony* (1963).[1] The Kaddish is a Jewish form of music, a Hebrew paean to God. This form Bernstein (1918-1990) has absorbed into his modern unbelief. Now in contrast to the original Kaddish, this one indicates that we can know nothing of what is there but can only listen to the musician, for he will make something of god for us. In this modern Kaddish the concert hall is "the sacred house," and in it the artist will "continue to create you, Father, and you, me." Art is seen as the one surviving miracle god has left.

The reviewer Leonard Marcus, in an early 1965 issue of *High Fidelity Magazine*, rightly concludes his review in this way: "Theologians have always had artists to bridge the gap to their flock. Now, for better or worse, the antitheologian has a powerful, artistic statement." Marcus correctly brings together the new secular mysticism and the new theology. There is no certainty that a god is there, but the poet, musician, or art as art is the prophet where there is no certainty about anything.

We should love good art. But art as art does not have the right to speak *ex cathedra* regardless of content.

There was a very interesting profile of John Cage (1912-1992) in the *New Yorker*,[2] part of which we shall quote in considering his music. The profile says: "[What] he is proposing is, essentially, the complete overthrow of the most basic assumptions of Western art since the Renaissance." We have already seen that the young person caught in the modern generation is 400 years away from the previous generation. So Cage is seeking to overthrow a total concept stretching right back at least through those 400 years to the Renaissance. The article goes on to say what it is he is smashing:

> The power of art to communicate ideas and emotions, to organize life into meaningful patterns, and to realize universal truths through the self-expressed individuality of the artist are only three of the assumptions that Cage challenges. In place of a self-expressive art created by the imagination, tastes, and desires of the artist, Cage proposes art born of chance and indeterminacy.

If God exists and we are made in his image, we can have real meaning, and we can have real knowledge through what he has communicated to us. If this is taken away, we are left only with man and his finite self-expression. At this point all one has is the expression of the individual man. But Cage quite logically sees that this will not do, and so he carries man's dilemma further, smashes self-expression and leaves chance speaking. This is the basis of his music. The article continues:

> A number of painters, writers, and composers in various countries have been moving in roughly the same direction in recent years, and many of them have used chance methods as a means to that end.

It names the Frenchman Pierre Boulez and the American Jackson Pollock. In the last stage of his painting Jackson Pollock (1912-1956) put his canvases horizontally on the floor and dripped paint on them by chance. After doing this for some time he felt he had exhausted the chance method. This left him no way to go on further, so he committed suicide. The article continues:

> Painters like the late Jackson Pollock in America and Georges Mathieu, in France, whose goal was and is certainly not anonymity,

have nevertheless sought in the accidents of throwing or dripping paint a key to creation beyond the reach of the artist's conscious mind and will.

In other words, this is not merely self-expression; it is in the same direction as Paul Klee's art—the hope that through the art form the impersonal universe will somehow speak as the artist works. The *New Yorker* profile continued:

Then just as he was beginning to feel ready to stop what he called "window-shopping" among the world's philosophies and religions, he discovered Zen-Buddhism. Dr. Daisetz T. Suzuki, the first important spokesman for Zen in the West, had recently come to America and was giving weekly lectures at Columbia University that were attended by psychoanalysts, scientists, painters, sculptors, and philosophy students. They were also attended by Cage. . . . By a rare coincidence, Cage found this Oriental idea perfectly summed up in the words of seventeenth-century English music commentator Thomas Mace, who once wrote that the function of music was "to sober and quiet the mind, thus rendering it susceptible to divine influences."

However, it is important to note that when Mace wrote this in the seventeenth century, he had the idea not only that music would quieten the mind but that afterwards the personal God could speak to it. God was really speaking. Cage, on the other hand, had come to the point where there is nobody there to speak to him. This is the fundamental distinction. Notice how clearly this comes across in a later section of the article:

One day, young Wolff brought a copy of an ancient Chinese book—the "I Ching" or "Book of Changes," which Pantheon had just published in an English translation. "The moment I opened the book and saw the charts and the hexagrams that were used for obtaining oracles according to the tossing of coins or yarrow sticks, I saw a connection with the charts I had been using," Cage says. "It was immediately apparent to me that I could derive a means of composing from these operations, and right then and there I sketched out the whole procedure for my 'Music of Changes,' which took its title from the book. I ran over to show the plan to Morty Feldman, who had rented a studio in the same building, and I can still remember him saying, 'You've hit it.'"

Back in the Chinese culture long ago, the Chinese had worked out a system of tossing coins or yarrow sticks by means of which the spirits would speak. The complicated method which they developed made sure that the person doing the tossing could not allow his own personality to intervene. Self-expression was eliminated so that the spirits could speak.

Cage picks up this same system and uses it. He too seeks to get rid of any individual expression in his music. But there is a very great difference. As far as Cage is concerned, there is nobody there to speak. There is only an impersonal universe speaking through blind chance.

Cage began to compose his music through the tossing of coins. It is said that for some of his pieces, lasting only twenty minutes, he tossed the coin thousands of times. This is pure chance, but apparently not pure enough; he wanted still more chance. So he devised a mechanical conductor. It was a machine working on cams, the motion of which could not be determined ahead of time, and the musicians followed that. Or as an alternative to this, sometimes he employed two conductors who could not see each other, both conducting simultaneously—anything, in fact, to produce pure chance. But in Cage's universe nothing comes through in the music except noise and confusion or total silence. All this is below the line of anthropology. Above the line there is nothing personal, only the philosophic other, or the impersonal everything.

There is a story that once, after the musicians had played Cage's total chance music, as he was bowing to acknowledge the applause, there was a noise behind him. He thought it sounded like steam escaping from somewhere, but then to his dismay realized it was the musicians behind him who were hissing. Often his works have been booed. However, when the audience boo at him they are, if they are modern men, in reality booing the logical conclusion of their own position as it strikes their ears in music.

Cage himself, however, is another example of a man who cannot live with his own conclusions. He says that the truth about the universe is a totally chance situation. You must just live with it and listen to it; cry if you must, swear if you must, but listen and go on listening.

Towards the end of the *New Yorker* profile we read this:

In 1954... the sculptor David Weinrib and his wife moved into an old farmhouse on a tract of land in Stony Point, Rockland County, forty miles from New York, which the Williamses had bought. Cage lived and worked in an attic room that he shared with a colony of wasps, and often took long, solitary walks in the woods. His eye was caught right away by the mushrooms that grew so abundantly in Rockland County, in all shapes, and sizes and brilliant colors. He started to collect books on mushrooms and to learn everything he could about them, and he has been doing so ever since. After all, mushroom hunting is a decidedly chancy, or indeterminate pastime.

No matter how much mycology one knows—and Cage is now one of the best amateur mycologists in the country, with one of the most extensive private libraries ever compiled on the subject—there is always the possibility of a mistake in identification. "I became aware that if I approached mushrooms in the spirit of my chance operations, I would die shortly," Cage said not long ago. "So I decided that I would not approach them in this way!"

In other words, here is a man who is trying to teach the world what the universe intrinsically is and what the real philosophy of life is, and yet he cannot even apply it to picking mushrooms. If he were to go out into the woods and begin picking mushrooms by chance, within a couple of days there would be no Cage!

We have said before that the ideas of modern people are destroying what "man" is in himself. But not only that, their views cut right across what the existence of the form and structure of the external universe indicates as well. As we see in the dilemma of Cage and his mushrooms, they cannot live on the basis of a consistent application of their views in regard to the universe, any more than they can in regard to man.

However, while Cage is forced into a hopeless dichotomy with his mushrooms, with his music he has continued to live consistently with his position, even though his music is nothing more than noise or silence. He has resisted the pressure to dress up impersonal Being in connotation words or sounds. Most modern men have not had this much courage.[3]

Mysticism in Literature—Henry Miller

In the writing of his earlier books, Miller (1891-1980) had not just set forth something which is dirty in a trivial sense, but he had succeeded in murdering everything which is meaningful, including sexual things. In these books he expressed his antilaw position, in every sense. However, Miller is another man who could not stand by his own position. Many others have been destroyed in their inner lives by his books, but he was not able to be so tough-fibered. So he joins the growing list of modern men who have accepted the new mysticism. In his later life Miller held to a pantheistic view of the world.

His later views are very cogently and consistently expressed in the preface which he wrote to the French edition of Elie Favre's *History of Art*. He calls his preface "A Sense of Wonder."[4] This is an important title, for it implies that he is going to contrast the "sense of wonder" with the intellect. And this in fact is what he does. For example he says, "Above all, he [Elie Favre] was a devout worshipper of the creative spirit in man. His approach, like our own Walt Whitman's, was nothing less than cosmic." This already has a pantheistic ring about it. Later on he continues, "What impact his work may have today, particularly on the young who are almost immune to wonder and mystery because of all the knowledge which has been crammed into their heads, I do not know." This is a significant sentence because he has set the intellect and knowledge against the sense of wonder. One's intellect would lead one only to the lower story of rationality and logic where there is no meaning in life, only machines. But in contrast to this one has a sense of wonder which bypasses the rational, and this sense is very much related to the use of the word *awe* that is so much in vogue today. The intellect is divorced and rejected.

A swift glance at Miller's introduction might lead the reader to think that he had suddenly become a Christian. He uses words and phrases which sound so correct. Thus, "In investing himself (man) with the powers of a god, man has divorced himself from God—and from the universe as well. That which was his inheritance, his gift and salvation, he has vitiated through pride and arrogance of intellect. He has not only turned his back on the source, he is no longer aware that there is a source, the source from which, as the Good Book says, all blessings flow."

It sounds most credible, and there is more to come: "The spirit which first breathed upon the waters will create anew. . . . There is no last word, unless it be the Word itself: 'In the beginning was the Word, and the Word was with God, and the Word was God.'" We are forced on the basis of this to ask, "Is Henry Miller one of us?" But the answer, which is negative, can be gleaned from a full reading of what he has said in this preface.

He says, "It forces me, the knowledge of this truth, to observe as I have again and again that behind all creation, whether human or divine, lies an impenetrable mystery. All those epoch-making names which he [Favre] reels off in his works, devastating forces when one thinks on it, because forces for good and evil simultaneously, all bear witness to the inexhaustible energy which invests even the tiniest particle of matter and demonstrate in miraculous everyday fashion that what is called matter or substance is but the adumbration of a luminous reality too powerful for our feeble senses to apprehend." There is a strong connection here with what Salvador Dali says concerning the dematerializing of the universe.

A little further on he writes, "It is only embryonic man to be sure who is staging this drama of annihilation." (The preceding context shows that what he is speaking of is the dropping of the atomic bomb.) "The true self is indestructible." You may think that he is referring to the individual soul here, but it is not so. He continues, "Art more than religion offers us the clue to life," and at the beginning of the preface, "Did he [Walt Whitman] not say somewhere that religions are born from art and not vice-versa?" We can link this statement with what Heidegger says about the poet: *just listen* to the poet. Miller tells us to look at art and not to worry about the content; art as art is the new prophet. "Art more than religion offers us the clue to life, but only to those who practice it, those who dedicate themselves, and who come ultimately to realize that they are but the humble instruments whose privilege it is to unveil the glory and the splendor of life." Rationality brings one to the content of Miller's books, *The Tropic of Cancer* and *The Tropic of Capricorn* and the rest. Therefore the intellect and knowledge must be put aside and a leap made into contentless mysticism and awe.

But the man who has arrived at this point does not really matter anyway. "What matters, in the ultimate, if for a few aeons of time this creature called man remains in abeyance, absent from the scene?" In other words, go ahead and drop the bomb, what does it matter?

The usual way of thinking, as exhibited by the shock shown following the publication of Nevil Shute's book *On the Beach* would be: if everybody is going to be annihilated tomorrow, what is the use of writing a poem or making a painting today? But Henry Miller and his new pantheistic mysticism would claim that it would not matter if tomorrow the oceans were calm and there were no man on the shore. *Individual* man does not matter.

However, he goes on to say, "This is an end, one of many—not *the* end. What man is in essence can never be destroyed. The spirit which first breathed upon the waters will create anew." He is not speaking of a personal God. He is using these connotation words to speak of pantheistic cycles. Everything, including human history, is being viewed as a series of cycles. What happens to the individuals does not matter, the cycles roll on! This is a thoroughgoing pantheistic idea. The man who can never be destroyed is not individual man, but just Man springing from the universe of what is. "Man, this embryonic form of a being which has neither beginning nor end, will give way to man again. Present-day man, the man of history, need not and will not be the last word. There is no last word, unless it is the Word itself. 'In the beginning was the Word, and the Word was with God, and the Word was God.' "

To Miller the world can be conceived of only in pantheistic terms, in endless cycles which repeat themselves. But in order to give it a personal sound, he uses biblical terms and phrases. In this way he utilizes the connotation attached to these forms, which comes out of the history of our race, to heighten the feeling of the semantic mysticism he has accepted.

The preface is concluded with these words: "Let us therefore, in reviewing this vast panorama of human achievement, think less of what was accomplished by the giants who parade throughout these volumes and more of the imperishable energy of which they were the fiery sparks. All may be lost, all forgotten, if only we remember that nothing is lost, nothing ever forgotten. 'As it was in the beginning, is now, and ever shall be: world without end.' " And with this devastating blow at the individual, who counts as nothing except as a part of the energy of the universe to which he is united as a spark to the fire, Miller finishes his preface.

It must be plain that the later Henry Miller cannot in any sense be called a Christian. He is doing the same as Salvador Dali and the new theologians are doing—namely, using Christian symbols to give an illusion of meaning to an impersonal world which has no real place for man.

This is Henry Miller, the writer of *The Tropics*, who in this preface takes up basically the same position as the new theologians. We have ample warning not to accept the "god words" of many modern theologians without being certain that they, like Henry Miller, are not using these words to give an *illusion* of meaning.

5
The Next Phase of Modern Theology

God Is Dead—Or Almost So!
It should be quite clear by this time that the mysticism of the new theology does not separate it from the intellectual climate of the second half of the twentieth century. Rather, it once more relates the new theology to the surrounding secular climate and consensus, because, as we have seen, the parallel secular semantic mysticisms are found in every one of the steps in the line of despair—philosophy, art, music and the general culture.

The new theology itself has an internal problem through separating the "upstairs" and "downstairs" into such watertight compartments. It came to this position:

Faith = No rationality; i.e., no contact with the cosmos (science) or history

---

All rationality—including scientific evidence and history

The tension is very strong because such a total antithesis between rationality and "religious values" destroys the unity of the individual man, and he becomes divided within himself. This gave rise to a deep-seated restlessness amongst many of the modern theologians. A new attempt was made to breach the dichotomy. This attempt took two forms: one form is to try to find a unity of the whole on the level of the lower story, the other on the level of the upper.

The first form was widely publicized as the "God is dead" theology. Its adherents chose the downstairs as a place to find a unity, and they have dispensed with God altogether, including the term *God.* When the real God-is-dead men say God is dead, they do not merely mean that God is being listened to very little in our modern secular world, *but that he never existed.* They put their emphasis on the lower story and seem to deny the validity of the upper story altogether. This leaves only the word *Jesus* downstairs. But we must be careful not to get caught out, for if we turn our backs for a moment these men use the word *Jesus* as a banner with *upper-story* overtones. We will represent it like this:

God is dead	
God is dead	Jesus......

These men chose to call themselves "Christian atheists." They are atheists in the classical sense of that word; and they are Christians only in the sense that they have adopted for themselves Bonhoeffer's definition of Christ, "The man for others." They really differ little from today's optimistic humanists.

This is fairly straightforward; in one sense these men are no longer "having their cake and eating it too." They lost all connotation words except the term *Jesus Christ,* and even this, to the extent to which they defined it, they have ruined as a connotation word. But they were not being left quiet in their atheism. The upper-story men who still want to keep the use of the connotation words fought back.

In actual fact this theology has a dead god in both the upper and lower stories:

The new mysticism—all knowledge concerning God is dead, any concept of a personal God is dead—therefore God is dead

On the basis of rationality God is dead

A typical exponent of the upper-story mentality was Paul Tillich (1886-1965). When asked at Santa Barbara, shortly before he died, if he ever prayed, he said, "No, but I meditate."

Thus in the upper story it is not only that *man* becomes a "shade," but the god of the new mysticism is no more than a mist which becomes only Being or Pan-everything. If we look at the theologians operating in this upper story, we may say that they are either atheists in the classical sense, or pantheists—depending on how one looks at it. Thus their god is also dead.

This vague pantheism, which we have noted in secular thinking also, creates problems for those brought up within the Christian faith. Thus for example, Bishop Robinson, a British theologian, in his writing insisted that God is actually transcendental after all. He spoiled it, however, when he went on to say that man is transcendental too (which, fascinatingly enough, is the exact word Sir Julian Huxley used about man), for this therefore means that "transcendental" really equals "nontranscendental," and we are back at square one.

When the theologians and the secular men use this word *transcendental*, I would suggest that they mean by it the things that surprise them when they examine man, things they could not expect to find on the basis of what they believe about man's origin. Or again, it means little more than Henry Miller's "sense of wonder." So when they use this word without definition, it does not thereby mean that they have escaped from the charge of pantheism.

As far as God and man are concerned, modern theology then is like this:

Nonrational, nonlogical faith =	No categories for God, all knowledge concerning God is dead. The personal God is dead. No categories for man or his meaning.

All rationality; i.e., all contacts with the cosmos (science), all contacts with history =	God is dead and man is a machine

A Quest by the Upper-Story Men
This position is a high price to pay for rejecting historic Christianity,

the Christianity of the Scripture and the Creeds. But instead of returning to the biblical position, they are making a further attempt to solve their difficulties apart from it. The next move was an attempt by the upper-story men to put a toe back into history.

Karl Barth, who can be said to be the inaugurator of all this, felt the need to try to hold back from the logical extension of his position developed by his followers. In his last years he spoke of a historic resurrection of Christ. It is not quite as simple as that, however; for on the presuppositions of these theologians, the Bible contains historical and scientific errors. Thus dichotomy, a divided concept of truth, is necessarily central in their concept of "religious truth."

They cannot go back to the old liberalism—there can be no going back to the old quest for the historical Jesus, for it failed. However, if they give up the division of truth *(which has been their answer to the old liberalism when it failed)*, then they have to face again what the older liberalism faced: on the one side nihilism (God is dead, man is dead and meaning is dead); on the other side, the answer of the historic and Reformation Christian position which states that there is a personal God, that man is made in his image, that he has communicated to his creature by a propositional, verbalized revelation of content, and thus this is able to be considered by the whole man. Or to put it very briefly, the only way out of their dilemma is to move back to the methodology of antithesis. Until they do this, no amount of talk about a physical resurrection of Christ will touch the heart of the discussion.[1]

This need to get a toe back into history by the upper-story men was ably dealt with in an article in *The Listener*, April 12, 1962, by Dr. John Macquarrie, then lecturer in Systematic Theology at Glasgow University, later at Union Theological Seminary, New York. We quote a relevant part of it. The article is called "History and the Christ of Faith":

A NEW QUEST

It should not surprise anybody that some of Bultmann's disciples, afraid of losing themselves in a world of myth and make-believe, have turned again to the question of the historical Jesus. Günther Bornkamm, for instance, says that "we must look for the history in the Kerygma" and that we should not be resigned or skeptical about the historical Jesus. Does this mean that we must reopen the interminable arguments as to whether this incident or that saying took place as recorded? It cannot mean this, for the earlier quest of the historical Jesus showed that no clear answers are to be had. The new quest is intended to be different; but unfortunately there is a good deal of confusion among those who have embarked on it as to what is intended, and Bultmann himself has been severely critical of some of them. He is content to hold that our knowledge is confined to the bare fact that there was a Jesus who was crucified, and does not extend to the manner of his life or personality.

My own view is that the Christian theologian needs to assert a minimal core of factual history if the Kerygma is to present us with a way of life that is realistic and not culled from a dream world. This minimal core is not a short list of essential incidents or sayings, but simply the *assertion* that at the source of the Christian religion there was an actual historical instance of the pattern of life proclaimed in the Kerygma.[2]

Here Dr. John Macquarrie acknowledges that the theologians cannot go back to the old liberal exhaustive search for the historical Jesus, for that ended in total failure. His own solution is the *assertion* that Jesus lived such and such a life. In other words, just say it is so.

There are two main attempts by the upper-story theologians to get a toe back into history in order not to lose themselves and God "in a world of myth and make-believe."

First, there is the use of the phrase "God's saving acts in history." This sounds very fine. But they do not mean by this that God has literally entered our space-time world at a particular point in order to begin and complete man's salvation. They mean that God is in some way saving or redeeming *all* history, including the most grisly acts of sin and cruelty which have been committed by individuals or groups.

Second, they just use the *word* "history"—this can take several forms. Macquarrie says that we must assert that certain events are history. The events are chosen arbitrarily and, of course, are not open to real historical inquiry. Or else they use the Bible as a vehicle for continuous existential experiences. They say such experiences did happen back in Bible times, but the way they are expressed in the Bible has no necessary relationship to the way the experience occurred. The biblical accounts are just the faulty cultural expression of that day. This way of looking at history is closely related to what the new Heidegger said about the mystique of language. These new theologians, both Protestants and some in the Roman Catholic Church, attempt therefore to manipulate biblical language as a help towards present existential experience.[3]

To these men language is always an interpretation, and therefore the words of the Bible are already an interpretation of the unknowable thing which occurred. The upper-story men are left with a flood of words.

Thus neither the lower-story men nor the upper-story men did very well in trying to ease the tension. But we can be sure the hopeless attempts will continue, for on one hand their dichotomy is uncomfortable in the extreme, and on the other hand they must keep it because this division of truth is the essence of the new theology.

Today's Opportunity for the New Theology

In spite of the confusion among the new theologians and in spite of the fact that they are not really saying anything unique among the secular mysticisms which surround us, yet there are reasons why this is a moment of opportunity for the new theology to take a privileged place in our culture, a place theology has not enjoyed for a long time. It could become a leader in tomorrow's affairs.

For some time society has been in danger of losing all sociological form. Men are facing a society without structure, and they want to fill the void that has appeared. For a long time Reformation ideas formed the basis of north European culture, and this extended to include that of the United States and English-speaking Canada, etc. But today that has been destroyed by the relativism both inside and outside the churches. Hence historic Christianity is now a minority group. Even the memory of past cultural forms is becoming weak. Moreover, the structural form of northern Europe is not the only one which is being battered to pieces. For example, one can see that Marxist Russia is moving in the same direction though at a slower rate because of its totalitarian controls. That is why modern Russian artists are being prevented from speaking freely, for they are carrying the modern thinking into Russian life.

Society cannot function without form and motivation. As the old sociological forms have been swept away, new ones must be found or society breaks down altogether. Sir Julian Huxley stepped in at this point with his suggestion that religion has a real place in modern society. But, he contended, it must be understood that religion is always evolving and that it needs to come under the control of society.

This suggestion is not as ridiculous as it sounds, even coming from a convinced humanist, if one understands the mentality of our age. The prevailing dialectical methodology fits itself easily into religious forms. After all, Senghor has said that on the basis of dialectical thinking his country would follow Teilhard de Chardin. It is well to remember that now men think dialectically on *both* sides of the Iron Curtain.

Teilhard de Chardin, incidentally, illustrates that "the progressive" Roman Catholic theologians are further away from historic Reformation Christianity than classical Roman Catholicism, because they are also dialectical thinkers.

The orthodox Roman Catholic would have told me that I was bound for hell because I rejected the true Church. He was dealing with a concept of absolute truth. But the new Roman Catholic who sits at my fireside says, "You are all right, Dr. Schaeffer, because you are so sincere." In the new Roman Catholicism such a statement often means that the dialectical method has taken over.

Therefore we are not surprised to find that the new Heidegger has followers, such as Karl Rahner, among some of the leading progressive Roman Catholic thinkers; and others such as Hans Küng have been strongly influenced by neo-orthodoxy. It is important to note that the position on Scripture by the Vatican Council shifted in the same direction, and men such as Raymond Panikkar,[4] Dom Bede Griffiths, O.S.C.,[5] and Anthony de Mello, S.J.,[6] are proclaiming a synthesis between Roman Catholicism and Hinduism. Truly these men have come a long way, but it is not in the direction of biblical Christianity. Neal Ascherson, under the dateline April 29, 1967, reported in a

London newspaper the conversations at Marienbad between the Paulus Society, which follows Karl Rahner, and Roger Garaudy, who was chief theoretician of the French Communist Party. He showed a streak of genius when he used the heading: "This Year in Marienbad—Where Marxist and Catholic Meet," thus relating this dialogue to the loss of categories as it was stressed by the film *The Last Year at Marienbad.*

The time, therefore, does seem right for this new theology to give the needed sociological forms and motivations. Of course, society could look elsewhere amongst the secular mysticisms for a new evolving religion, but the new theology has some strong advantages.

First, the undefined connotation words that the new theology uses are deeply rooted in our Western culture. This is much easier and more powerful than using new and untraditional words.

Second, these men control many of the large denominations of Protestantism, and if the progressives in the Roman Catholic Church consolidate their position, that Church as well. The liberal Roman Catholic theologians already have great influence in the Roman Catholic Church, and they use it widely. This gives the liberal theologians the advantage of functioning within the organizational stream of the Church, and thus both its organization and linguistic continuity is at their disposal.

Third, people in our culture in general are already in process of being accustomed to accept nondefined, contentless religious words and symbols, without any rational or historical control. Such words and symbols can be filled with the content of the moment. The words *Jesus* and *Christ* are the most ready for the manipulator. The phrase *Jesus Christ* has become a contentless banner which can be carried in any direction for sociological purposes. In other words, because the phrase *Jesus Christ* has been separated from true history and the content of Scripture, it can be used to trigger religiously motivated sociological actions directly contrary to the teaching of Christ. This is already in evidence, as for example in the "new" morality being advocated by many within the church today.

So there is open to the new theology the possibility of supplying society with an endless series of religiously motivated arbitrary absolutes. It is against such manipulated semantic mysticism that we do well to prepare ourselves, our children and our spiritual children.

Section 3

How Historic
Christianity Differs
from the
New Theology

1
Personality or a Devilish Din

Our forefathers used the term *systematic theology* to express their view that Christianity is not a series of isolated religious statements, but that it has a beginning and flows on to an end. Each part relates to each other part and to the whole, and to what stands first in the system. It is perfectly possible that such a systematic understanding of Christianity can become a dead thing, but let us not despise the word *systematic* as if it were automatically a corpse.

Rightly understood, Christianity as a system has the answers to the basic needs of modern man. In this it differs from the new theology, which has no adequate basis upon which to give answers which will stand up to the test of rationality and the whole of life as we must live it.

The first basic need is caused by the lack of certainty regarding the reality of individual personality. Every man is in tension until he finds a satisfactory answer to the problem of who he himself is.

The biblical Christian answer takes us back first to the very beginning of everything and states that personality is intrinsic in what is—not in the pantheistic sense of the universe being the extension of the essence of God (or what is), but that a God who is personal on the high order of Trinity created all else. Within the Trinity, before the creation of anything, there was real love and real communication.[1] Following on from this statement the Bible states that this God who is personal created man in his own image. A personal God created all things freely in a nondeterminate fashion, and man is created in a special situation—what I would call a special circle of creation. He is the image of this kind of God, and so personality is intrinsic to his makeup. God is personal, and man is also personal.

It might be helpful to illustrate the situation in this way. Imagine you are in the Alps, and from a high vantage point you can see three parallel ranges of mountains with two valleys in between. In one valley there is a lake, but the other is dry. Suddenly you begin to witness what sometimes happens in the Alps—a lake forming in the second valley where there was none before. As you see the water rising, you may wonder what its source is. If it stops at the same level as the lake in the neighboring valley, you may, after careful measurements, conclude that there is a possibility that the water has come from the first valley. But if your measurement shows that the level of the second lake is twenty feet higher than the first, then you can no longer consider that its source may be from the neighboring valley, and you would have to seek another explanation. Personality is like that; no one has ever thought of a way of deriving personality from nonpersonal sources.

Therefore, biblical Christianity has an adequate and reasonable explanation for the source and meaning of human personality. Its source is sufficient—the personal God on the high order of Trinity. Without such a source men are left with personality coming from the impersonal (plus time, plus chance).

The two alternatives are very clear-cut. Either there is a personal beginning to everything, or one has what the impersonal throws up by chance out of the time sequence. The fact that the second alternative may be veiled by connotation words makes no difference. The words used by Eastern pantheism; the theological words such as Tillich's "Ground of Being"; the secular shift from mass to energy or motion—all eventually come back to the impersonal, plus time, plus chance. If *this* is really the only answer to man's personality, then personality is no more than an illusion, a kind of sick joke which no amount of semantic juggling will alter. Only some form of mystical jump will allow us to accept that personality comes from impersonality.

This was the position into which Teilhard de Chardin was forced. His answer is only a mystical answer of words.

Because these men will not accept the only explanation which can fit the facts of their own experience, they have become metaphysical magicians. No one has presented an idea, let alone demonstrated it to be feasible, to explain how the impersonal beginning, plus time, plus chance, can give personality. We are distracted by a flourish of endless words, and lo, personality has appeared out of the hat! This is the water rising above its source. No one in all the history of humanistic, rationalistic thought has found a solution. As a result, either the thinker must say man is dead, because personality is a mirage; or else he must hang his reason on a hook outside the door and cross the threshold into the leap of faith which is the new level of despair.

A man like Sir Julian Huxley has clarified the dilemma by acknowledging, though he is an atheist, that somehow or other, against all that one might expect, man functions better if he acts as though God is there. This sounds like a feasible solution for a moment, the kind of answer a computer might give if you fed the sociological data into it. God is dead, but act as if he were alive. However, a moment's reflection will show what a terrible solution this is. Ibsen, the Norwegian, put it like this: if you take away a man's lie, you take away his hope.[2] These thinkers are saying in effect that man can function as man for an extended period of time only if he acts on the assumption that a lie (that the personal God of Christianity is there) is true. You cannot find any deeper despair than this for a sensitive person. This is not an optimistic, happy, reasonable or brilliant answer. It is darkness and death.

Imagine that a universe existed which was made up only of liquids and solids, and no free gases. A fish was swimming in this universe. This fish, quite naturally, was conformed to its environment, so that it was able to go on living. But let us suppose that by blind chance, as the evolutionists would have us believe, this fish developed lungs as it continued swimming in this universe without any gases. Now this fish would no longer be able to function and fulfill its position as a fish. Would it then be higher or lower in its new state with lungs? It would be lower, for it would drown. In the same way, if man has been kicked up by chance out of what is only impersonal, then those things that make him man—hope of purpose and significance, love, motions of morality and rationality, beauty and verbal communication—are ultimately unfulfillable and are thus meaningless. In such a situation, is man higher or lower? He would then be the lowest creature on the scale. The green moss on the rock is higher than he, for it can be fulfilled in the universe which exists. But if the world is what these men say it is, then man (not only individually but as a race), being unfulfillable, is dead. In this situation man should not walk on the grass, but respect it—for it is higher than he!

The Logical End of Denying Personality

In the 1960s while I was giving a series of lectures at an American college, I received an anonymous note from one of the students. This note read: "A question I would like you to answer on one of your broadcast talks if you could: with reference to what you have said about some artists destroying man, what should I do? I *want* to destroy too." Many of the students of the 1960s sought to destroy (as the Punks do in the 1980s). And if the smashing of things stops, and people come to the conclusion that there are no better answers than they have been given, the general apathy of the later 1970s and the early 1980s dominates.

In face of this modern nihilism, smashing or the apathy, Christians are often lacking in courage. We tend to give the impression that we will hold on to the outward forms whatever happens, even if God really is not there. But the opposite ought to be true of us, so that people can see that we demand the truth of what is there and that we are not dealing merely with platitudes. In other words, it should be understood that we take this question of truth and personality so seriously that if God were not there, we would be among the first to have the courage to step out of the queue. Insofar as we show this to be our attitude, maybe the far-out ones will begin to take us seriously and listen to what we have to say. If they do not see that in our integrity we would join with them in destruction, "dropping out" or apathy, except that we know we have an adequate basis for personality and the reality of morals, then they will not and should not listen to us.

According to the tape recording of my lecture that night in the 1960s, my answer to the student who said that he or she wanted to destroy was: "I would say to you tonight that if we live in this intrinsically impersonal world, dress it up if you will with the word *pantheism*, either in the Eastern thought or in the new theology, or if I speak of it in secular terms, if this is what I am, and all men are, with their aspirations, if this is all they are, unfulfillable products of chance, a sterile sport, then come beside me, because I wish to destroy too. If indeed these ideas are your ideas, you should stand beside such a man to destroy. If I am an artist, I should wish to destroy. I should say with the Dutch artist Karel Appel, 'I do not paint, I hit.' I should say with John Cage, 'It is only chance,' with a resultant noise and a devilish din. But further, let us understand, in such a case, what love will mean. Love will mean facing the problem of pushing the button that destroys the human race. This is the distinction between there being a real meaning of personality that makes it reasonable to love and have compassion, a real reason to keep humanity alive; and no real meaning, and therefore a love resulting in that which should destroy. This then would be nearer to the truth of what is, and what will eventually happen, not only to the individual, but to the human race.

"This person who wrote this note understands something. In such a case I would ask him to come to my side and destroy, but I would ask him also to be honest in considering the other possibility, that all this is not so, but rather that we started with a personal beginning and therefore there is intrinsic meaning to personality, my personality, and other men's personality in this universe. This is the distinction between the two positions. The things we have considered are not only theoretical things—they are things that cut down into the warp and woof of the understanding of life. We would say indeed to the man who would destroy a romantic concept which has no base, destroy it indeed. Demand a realistic answer. Here we stand face to face with the real issue of the new theology and the whole new thought."

This is the crux of the matter; either an intrinsically personal "what is," in the sense of a creation by the personal God, or John Cage's devilish din!

2
Verifiable Facts & Knowing

*I*n historic Christianity a personal God creates man in his own image, and in such a case there is nothing that would make it nonsense to consider that he would communicate to man in verbalized form. Why should he not communicate in verbalized form when he has made man a verbalizing being, in his thoughts as well as in communication with other men? Having created man in his own image, why should he fail to communicate to that verbalizing being in such terms? The communication would then be three ways: God to man, and vice versa; man to man; and man to himself. Someone may raise queries as to whether in fact such communication has taken place, but in this field of reference, it is neither a contradictory nor a nonsense statement. Such a concept would be nonsense if one had the presupposition of a totally closed field of cause and effect. But if you are a person who holds that cause and effect has been and is totally closed, then you need to ask if such a view as yours really stands up to all we know, and specifically whether your worldview explains why people verbalize to each other.

Why should God not communicate *propositionally* to the man, the verbalizing being, whom he made in such a way that we communicate propositionally to each other? Therefore, in the biblical position there is the possibility of verifiable facts involved: a personal God communicating in verbalized form propositionally to man—not only concerning those things man would call in our generation "religious truths," but also down into the areas of history and science.

God has set the revelation of the Bible in history; he did not give it (as he could have done) in the form of a theological textbook. Having set the revelation in history, what sense then would it make for God to give us a revelation in which the *history* was wrong? God has also set man in the *universe*, which the Scriptures themselves say speaks of this God. What sense then would it make for God to give his revelation in a book that was wrong concerning the universe? The answer to both questions must be, "No sense at all!"

It is plain, therefore, that from the viewpoint of the Scriptures themselves there is a unity over the whole field of knowledge. God has spoken, in a linguistic propositional form, truth concerning himself and truth concerning man, history and the universe.

Here is an adequate basis for the unity of knowledge. The unity encompasses both the upstairs and the downstairs. This is the answer to the discussion of the unity between nature and grace and modern man's question of knowledge above and below the line of anthropology. The unity is there because God has spoken truth into all areas of our knowledge.

At the same time one must avoid the opposite mistake of saying that because God has communicated truly concerning science, all scientific study is wasted. This is a false deduction. To say that God communicates *truly* does not mean that God communicates *exhaustively*. Even in our human relationships we never have exhaustive communication, though what we do have may be true. Thus, as far as our position in the universe is concerned, though the infinite God has said true things concerning the whole of what he has made, our knowledge is not thereby meant to be static. Created in his image, we are rational and, as such, we are able to, and intended to, explore and discover further truth concerning creation.

God says, in effect, "Learn of the truth that I have made in the external world." Finite man in the external universe, being finite, has no sufficient reference point if he begins absolutely and autonomously from himself; thus he needs *certain knowledge*. God gives us this in the Scriptures. With this in mind the scientist can understand, in their ultimate relationships, the truths that he is looking at. Thus scientific study in itself can be to the glory of God, for here man is functioning properly in the universe in which God has placed him. He is telling us what is truly there, and he is adding to the store of knowledge of his fellowmen.

The new theology cannot give an adequate framework for ascertaining facts and knowledge. It cannot because it removes the possibility of communication at the only two points that can be discussed and verified, namely, history and the universe. Religious truths cannot be discussed once they are divorced from the other two. Bezzant, in the book *Objections to Christian Belief*,[1] well illustrates how crucial this matter of truth is. Though Bezzant is an older type of liberal, and though the book is destructive in many ways, nevertheless he has seen this point very clearly. Having attacked the historic Christian position, he then suddenly swings around and trains all his guns on neo-orthodoxy: "When I am told that it is precisely its immunity from proof which secures the Christian proclamation from the charge of being mythological, I reply that immunity from proof can 'secure' nothing whatever except immunity from proof and call nonsense by its name." This is a tremendous sentence. At this point he has truly understood the fatal flaw of modern theology. It may dress up its position with all kinds of clothes, but it remains irrational and what it is talking about can never really be discussed, because it is no longer open to verification.

I remember hearing a speaker in England say at a conference at which we were both speaking, "Bultmann is infallible for twenty minutes each Sunday." That is, all the new theology can do is preach and ask the people to believe or not to believe, without the exercise of reason. In this way, man becomes *less than* the fallen man of the biblical Christian position.

The historic Christian answer concerning verifiable facts and knowing depends on who God is, on who is there. The God who is there according to the Scriptures is the personal-infinite God. There is no other god like this God. It is ridiculous to say that all religions teach the same things when they disagree at the fundamental point as to what God is like. The gods of the East are infinite by definition—the definition being "god is all that is." This is the pan-everythingism god. The gods of the West have tended to be personal but limited; such were the gods of the Greeks, Romans and Germans. But the God of the Bible, Old and New Testaments alike, is the infinite-personal God.

It is this God who has created various orders of creation, like this:

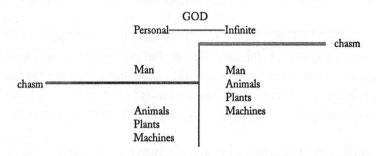

How then is God's creation related to himself and to itself? On the side of God's infinity there is a break between God and the whole of his creation. I am as separated from God in the area of his being the Creator and infinite, I being the creature and finite, as is the atom or energy particle. I am no closer to God on this side than the machine.

However, on the side of God's *personality*, the break comes between man and the rest of creation. In terms of modern thought this is a dynamic concept, of which modern man and modern theology know nothing. So Albert Schweitzer identified himself with the hippopotamus, for he did not understand that man's relationship is upward; and therefore he looked downward to a creature which does many of the same things as himself. But on the *side of personality*, if our relationship is upward, then everything concerning man's "mannishness" is in place.

The biblical Christian says that, on the side of personality, man can know God truly, though he cannot know God exhaustively. Unlike the new theology, he is not trapped by the two alternatives of knowing God completely or not knowing him at all. We are not shut up to a total comprehension of the infinite.

Modern man and the new theology have only this:

Infinite

=================== chasm

Man
Animal
Plant
Machine

Modern man has driven a wedge between the personal and the infinite and says that personality equals finiteness. He has equated personality with limitedness. But the Christian says that the only *limitation* which personality intrinsically must have is that it cannot be impersonal at the same time. To say that personality must always be limited in other ways is to try to make an absolute which one cannot make. Indeed, human personalities are limited in other ways, but this is because they are created and finite, not because they are personal.

Personality as Such Cannot Necessarily Imply Limitedness

A man from Israel who was an atheist wrote and asked me, "What sense does it make for a man to give his son to the ants, to be killed by ants, in order to save the ants?" I replied that it makes no sense at all for a man to give his son to the ants, to be killed by the ants, in order to save the ants, because man *as a personality* is totally separated from the ants. Man's only relation to the ants is in the areas of Being and creaturehood. However, in the area of personality man's relationship is upward to God, and therefore the incarnation and death of the Son of God for the sake of man's salvation are sensible.

The reasonableness of the incarnation and the reasonableness of communication between God and man turn on this point—that man, as man, is created in the image of God.

Divine and Human Communication

The communication which God has made to man is true, but that does not mean it is exhaustive. This is an important distinction which we must always bear in mind. To know anything exhaustively we would need to be infinite, as God is. Even in heaven we shall not be this.

God has communicated to man, not only about the cosmos and history but also about himself. And God's attributes so communicated are meaningful to God, the author of the communication, as well as to man, the recipient of the communication. What God has revealed concerning his attributes is not only meaningful below the line of anthropology. The line of anthropology is not a brazen heaven over our heads which cannot be penetrated. The God who has spoken is not the unknowable infinite above the line. The God who has created man in his own image communicates true truth about himself. Therefore this need not be thought of as only an existential experience or contentless "religious ideas." We have true knowledge, for as the Scriptures say so simply and overwhelmingly, when God wrote the Ten Commandments on stone,[2] or when Jesus spoke to Paul on the Damascus road in the Hebrew language,[3] a real language was used—subject to grammars and lexicons—a language to be understood.

When we talk to each other there are three theoretical possibilities in our exchange of words. The first is that we fail to communicate at all, probably because our backgrounds are too far apart. The second possibility is the very opposite of this: that when we use terms we all give to them exactly the same meaning, so that we understand each other exhaustively. Neither of these concepts stands careful analysis.

The weakness of saying that one is not able to communicate at all was shown up in a conversation I once had with an undergraduate at St. Andrews University in Scotland. Other students had said they found him difficult to talk to, that what he said did not seem to make sense, and they were at a loss to know where to start. I had half an hour to spend with him. After only two minutes of talking in his room, he said, "Sir, I don't think we are communicating." I started again. About two minutes later he repeated himself, "Sir, I don't think we are communicating." I began to think that the half-hour would be spent in a nonsense session! I looked down and noticed that he had very thoughtfully prepared a lovely tea. There it all was, pot of tea, cups and so on. So I said rather gruffly to him, "Give me some tea!" He was taken aback, but he passed me a cup, full of tea. Then I said, "Sir, I think we are communicating." From then on we had a very effective conversation.

The simple fact is that no one who takes the trouble to study linguistics really believes that just because we bring our own background to the words, idioms and phrases we use, we cannot communicate at all. On the other hand we need to be warned: just because we know what *we* mean by a term does not mean that the person to whom we speak understands precisely the same thing. That would be very naive. In human conversation we have true communication, but it is never exhaustive. This is the third and only realistic possibility in our speaking to one another.

If we transfer the possibility of communication from the realm of human intercourse to that of the Divine-human, then the same principle applies. The biblical presentation indicates that because man is made in God's image, the problem of God communicating to him is not of an absolutely different order from that of man speaking to man. We are finite, God is infinite, but we can understand truly.

Love Is More Than a Word

This conception of the way in which God communicates gives a world which is different from the one in which modern man is struggling. It means quite simply that man no longer needs to destroy, nor to sink into apathy; there is a reason to live, build and love. Man is no longer adrift. We may demonstrate how different the two worlds are by considering the meaning of love. Modern man quite properly considers the conception of love to be overwhelmingly important as he looks at personality. Nevertheless, he faces a very real problem as to the meaning of love. Though modern man tries to hang everything on the word *love*, love can easily degenerate into something very much less because he really does not understand it. He has no adequate universal for love.

On the other hand, the Christian does have the adequate universal he needs in order to be able to discuss the meaning of love. Among the things we know about the Trinity is that the Trinity was before the creation of everything else and that love existed between the persons of the Trinity before the foundation of the world.[4] This being so, the existence of love as we know it in our makeup does not have an origin in chance, but from that which has always been.

Above the line of anthropology, God the Father loved God the Son before the creation of the world—this is on a horizontal plane. On the vertical plane God also loves me, who am below the line of anthropology. The word and act of love has crossed the line of anthropology downward. Then, also on the vertical plane, I am to love God. The word and act of love has crossed the line of anthropology upward. Finally, I am commanded by God to love my wife, children, neighbors, below the line of anthropology. Here is the word and act of love horizontally below the line of anthropology.

The relationships of love can be shown like this:

Two things follow from this. First, I can know something truly of what it means when I am told that God the Father loves the Son. When I see a boy and a girl walking together arm in arm, obviously showing love towards each other, I do not know all that they feel towards one another; yet because I too love my woman, my looking at them is not as a dog would look at them. It is not exhaustive, but it is true understanding—there is true correlation. And when I talk about love existing in the Trinity before creation, I am not talking gibberish. Though I am very far from plumbing its depths when applied to God himself, yet the word *love* and the reality of love when Christ spoke of the Father loving him before the foundation of the world has true meaning for me.

Second, when I love my woman, its meaningfulness is not exhausted by the context of this one individual relationship alone, nor even the love of all men for all women, nor all finite love. The validity and meaning of love rest upon the reality that love exists between the

Father and Son in the Trinity. When I say I love, instead of this being a nonsense word, it has meaning. It is rooted in what has always been in the personal relationship existing in the Trinity before the universe was created. Man's love is not a product of chance that has no fulfillment in what has always been. Love is a thing not only of meaning but of beauty and wonder to be nourished in joy.

This then is the second great difference between Christianity and the new theology. The latter gives no basis for verifiable facts and knowing, including knowing the content of words used about God above the line of anthropology. Thus, such a word as *love* has no meaning or value beyond the realm of limited man. *It should be obvious by this time that Christianity and the new theology have no relationship except the use of a common terminology with different meanings.*

3
The Dilemma
of Man

We have considered two areas in which Christianity and the new theology fundamentally disagree—personality and knowledge. There is one more area where disagreement could not be more radical, and that is the question of man and his dilemma. Anyone with sensitivity and concern for the world can see that man is in a great dilemma. Man is able both to rise to great heights and to sink to great depths of cruelty and tragedy. Modern man is desperately struggling with the concept of man in his dilemma. Most of the paintings of the crucifixion today, Salvador Dali's for example, are not of Christ dying on the cross in history. They are using the Christ-symbol to exhibit man in agony.

Of course it is possible to try *not* to get involved in man's dilemma; but the only way not to get involved in the dilemma of man is by being young enough, well enough, having money enough and being egotistic enough to care nothing about other human beings.

As we consider this question of man and his dilemma, only two possible explanations can be given. The first explanation suggests a *metaphysical cause*. This says, in effect, that man's problem is that he is too small, too finite to wrestle with the factors that confront him. The second explanation is quite different; it puts man's dilemma down to a *moral cause*. If the first explanation is right, then one is bound to conclude that man has always been in the same dilemma. Thus, for example, the new theology says that man has always been fallen man. This also means that there is no moral answer to the problem of evil and cruelty. Because man, whether somehow created by a curious thing called god or kicked up out of the slime by chance, has always been in this dilemma, the dilemma is part of what being "man" is. And if this is what man intrinsically is, and he has always been like this, then the French art historian and poet Baudelaire is right when he says, "If there is a God, he is the Devil." This statement was simply the logical deduction from the premise that man, with all his cruelty and suffering, is now as he always has been. At this point Baudelaire was consistent and refused to give any kind of romantic alternatives as an explanation. But the Bible says that this is not the situation.

One day I was talking to a group of people in the room of a young South African in Cambridge University. Among others, there was present a young Indian who was of Sikh background but a Hindu by religion. He started to speak strongly against Christianity, but did not really understand the problems of his own beliefs. So I said, "Am I not correct in saying that on the basis of your system, cruelty and noncruelty are ultimately equal, that there is no intrinsic difference between them?" He agreed. The people who listened and knew him as a delightful person, an "English gentleman" of the very best kind, looked up in amazement. But the student in whose room we met, who had clearly understood the implications of what the Sikh had admitted, picked up his kettle of boiling water with which he was about to make tea, and stood with it steaming over the Indian's head. The man looked up and asked him what he was doing, and he said with a cold yet gentle finality, "There is no difference between cruelty and noncruelty." Thereupon the Hindu walked out into the night.

If the metaphysical explanation to man's dilemma is given, it is not an abstraction. In such a case, all that moves man at his best is really meaningless.

The Scandal of the Cross
There is a serious commentary given on man and his dilemma in

Albert Camus's book *The Plague*.[1] The story is about a plague brought by rats into the city of Oran at the beginning of the Second World War. On the surface it reads like an account of any city that might have been struck by such a tragedy. But Camus intends a deeper understanding. Therefore he confronts the reader with a serious choice: either he must join the doctor and fight the plague, in which case, says Camus, he will then also be fighting God; or he can join with the priest and not fight the plague, and thus be antihumanitarian. This is the choice; and this is the dilemma which Camus faced and which all those face who, like him, do not have the Christian answer.[2]

However, the new theology has no answer to the dilemma either. Its followers are caught equally in Camus' problem and Baudelaire's proposition. All that is reasonable in their position, based on observing the world as it is, says God is the Devil. Nevertheless, because they do not want to live with this conclusion, by an act of blind faith they say God is good. This, they say, is what the "scandal of the cross" is—to believe that God is good against all the evidence open to reason. But this is emphatically not the "scandal of the cross." The true scandal is that however faithfully and clearly one preaches the gospel, at a certain point the world, because it is in rebellion, will turn from it. Men turn away in order not to bow before the God who is there. This is the "scandal of the cross."

Modern theology may use the term *guilt*, but because it is not orientated in a true moral framework, it turns out to be no more than guilt-feelings. And as in their system they have no place for true guilt, the death of Jesus on the cross takes on an entirely different meaning. Following from this, the work of Christ and the ministry of the church becomes one of two things: either a basis for sociological motivation, using undefinable religious terms; or a means for psychological integration, again using religious words. In both cases, the connotation words used are open to the control of the manipulators.

There is an opposite danger: that the orthodox Christian will fail to realize that at times guilt-feelings are present when no true guilt exists. Let us remember that the Fall resulted in division not only between God and man, and man and man, but between man and himself. Hence there are psychological guilt-feelings without true guilt. In such cases we must show genuine compassion. But where there is a real moral guilt before the God who is there, this must never be passed off or explained away as psychological, as the new theology does.

Another result of the position of the new theology is that there is no personal antithesis at the point of justification. For the new theologians there can never be a qualitative difference in man's relationship to God. The Christian view is that when a person casts himself on Jesus Christ as Savior, at that moment he has passed from death to life, from the kingdom of darkness to the kingdom of God's dear Son.[3] Justification means to be acquitted from true guilt and no longer to be condemned. This is an absolute personal antithesis. If on the other hand, there is no absolute antithesis between moral and immoral, cruel and noncruel, then the only difference is a quantitative one.

We may not play with the new theology even if we may think we can turn it to our advantage. This means, for example, we must beware of cooperation in evangelistic enterprises which force us into a position of accepting the new theology as Christian. If we do this, we have cut the ground from under the biblical concept of the personal antithesis of justification.

Because the new theology has no place for antithesis, and because for its proponents sin and guilt are, in the last analysis, a metaphysical and not a moral problem, they have either an implicit or explicit universalism regarding man's ultimate salvation. It is naive for evangelicals to regard this universalism as merely an unrelated corner of the neo-orthodox system. It may not always be explicit in the teaching of the new theologians, but we must see that the logic of their view concerning man's dilemma irresistibly drives them to this position. At this point their beliefs hang together very well. They have no final antithesis between right and wrong; therefore there can be no such thing as true moral guilt; therefore justification as a radically changed relationship with God can have no meaning; therefore no one is finally condemned. On the basis of their system, this is a perfectly consistent and necessary position to hold. Universalism is naturally related to what their system is.

Historic Christianity and Man's Dilemma

The historic Christian position is that man's dilemma has a moral cause. God, being nondetermined, created man as a nondetermined person. This is a difficult idea for anyone thinking in twentieth-century terms because most twentieth-century thinking sees man as determined. He is determined either by chemical factors, as the Marquis de Sade held and Francis Crick is trying to prove, or by psychological factors, as Freud and others have suggested, or by sociological factors, such as B. F. Skinner holds. In these cases, or as a result of a fusion of them, man is considered to be programmed. If this is the case, then man is not the tremendous thing the Bible says he is, made in the image of God as a personality who can make a free first choice. Because God created a true universe outside of himself (not as an extension of his essence), there is a true history which exists. Man as created in God's image is therefore a significant man in a significant history, who can choose to obey the commandment of God and love him, or revolt against him.

This is the wonder of man and the wonder of history. It is the very opposite of the Zen Buddhist statement which says, "The mind of man is like the wind in a pine tree in a Chinese ink drawing." In this, man is killed twice. He is only the wind in the pine tree, and even then only in a drawing. Christianity teaches the very reverse of what the Eastern thinker says. Man can understand and respond to the One who, having made him and communicated with him, called upon him to show that he loved God by simple command: "Don't do this." The test could have been something else. No act of primitive magic is involved here. This is the infinite-personal God calling on personal man to act by choice. And it was a motivated command, "for in the day that you eat of it you shall surely die,"[4] which would make no sense if man is only a machine. He could so act by choice because he was created to be different from the animal, the plant and the machine.

To ask that man should have been made so that he *was not able to revolt* is to ask that God's creation should have ceased after he created plants and animals. It is to ask that man should be reduced to machine programming. It is to ask that man as man should not exist.

If one begins to consider the Christian system as a total system, one must begin with the infinite-personal triune God who is there, and who was communicating and loving before anything else was. If one begins to consider how sinful man can return to fellowship with God, one must begin with Christ, his person and work. But if one begins to consider the differences between Christianity and rationalistic philosophy's answers, one must begin by understanding that man and history are now abnormal. It is not that philosophy and Christianity deal with completely different questions, but that historic Christianity and rationalistic philosophy differ in their answers—including the important point as to whether man and history are now normal or abnormal. They also differ in that rationalistic thinking starts with only the knowledge finite man can glean for himself.[5]

Christianity says man is now abnormal—he is separated from his Creator, who is his only sufficient reference point—not by a metaphysical limitation but by true moral guilt. As a result he is now also separated from his fellowmen, and from himself. Therefore, when he is involved in cruelty, he is not being true to what he was initially created to be. Cruelty is a symptom of abnormality and a result of a moral, historic space-time Fall.

What does a historic space-time Fall involve? It means that there was a period before man fell; that if you had been there, you could have seen Adam before he fell; that at the point when he revolted against God by making a free choice to disobey God's commandment, there was a tick of the clock. Take away the first three chapters of Genesis, and you cannot maintain a true Christian position nor give Christianity's answers.

4
God's Answer to Man's Dilemma

With the Christian answer it is now possible to understand that there are true moral absolutes. There is no law behind God, because the furthest thing back is God. The moral absolutes rest upon God's character. The creation as he originally made it conformed to his character. The moral commands he has given to men are an expression of his character. Men as created in his image are to live by choice on the basis of what God is. The standards of morality are determined by what conforms to his character, while those things which do not conform are immoral.

God can know about things that are not actualized. For example, he knew all about Eve, but she was not actualized until he made her. The same thing can be true in the area of morals. When man sins, he brings forth what is contrary to the moral law of the universe and as a result he is morally and legally guilty. Because man is guilty before the Lawgiver of the universe, doing what is contrary to his character, his sin is significant and he is morally significant in a significant history. Man has true moral guilt. This is entirely different from the conception of modern thought, which states that actions do not lead to guilt—a view within which actions thus become morally meaningless. Even the most degraded actions of sin have no final moral meaning. Ultimately "good" and "bad" actions alike are zero. This is an important factor in modern man seeing man as zero.

The Christian answer begins by saying that man is a moral creature made in the image of the Creator, that there is a law in the universe which, if broken, means that man is culpable. In this view, man is morally significant both as far as God is concerned and as far as his fellowmen are concerned. The modern non-Christian answer denies the legitimacy of moral absolutes, refuses to make any kind of final moral comment on man's actions and thus reduces cruel and noncruel acts to the same level. With this answer not only is the concept of sin reduced to less than the biblical concept, but *man* is reduced to less than the biblical concept of guilty man.

If the modern explanation is accepted, then there ceases to be an answer to man's dilemma—man is as he was in the beginning and ever will be. With the moral (in contrast to the metaphysical) explanation of man's position in the universe and his consequent dilemma following the Fall, there is a possible solution.

If there is true moral guilt in the presence of a personal God (rather than a metaphysical intrinsic situation of what is and always has been), then perhaps there will be a solution from God's side. And God says to man that there is a solution. That solution rests upon God saying that he is holy and he is love, and in his love he has loved the world, and he sent his Son. Now in history, there on Calvary's cross, in space and time, Jesus died. And we should never speak of Jesus' death without linking it to his person. This is the eternal Second Person of the Trinity. When he died, with the division that man has caused by his revolt now carried up into the Trinity itself, there in expiation, in propitiation and substitution, the true moral guilt is met by the *infinite* value of Jesus' death. Thus Jesus says: "It is finished."

Romans 3:26 is a verse that we tend to pass by too quickly in the midst of the structure of the first three chapters of Romans. These chapters tell us first why man is lost, and then the solution in the propitiatory death of Jesus Christ. At this point Paul can say: "that he himself might be just and *yet* [the force of the Greek construction] the justifier of him who has faith in Jesus." On the one hand, because of the infinite value of Christ's death, God does not have to surrender his absolutely holy character; and on the other, he does not have to violate man's significance in order for him to be able to pardon guilt and restore man's broken relationship to himself. This is the very opposite of the denial of antithesis and significance in modern man's leap into the dark, which says that somehow we must believe, without reason, that God is love. A moral absolute remains, and yet there is a solution to man's dilemma.

There Need Be No Either-Or in *La Peste*

From the biblical answer flow four important facts.

First, the God who is there is a good God.

Second, there is a hope of a solution to the dilemma of man.

Third, there is a sufficient basis for morals. Nobody has ever discovered a way of having real "morals" without a moral absolute. If there is no moral absolute, we are left with hedonism (doing what I like) or some form of the social contract theory (what is best for society as a whole is right). However, neither of these alternatives corresponds to the moral motions that men have. Talk to people long enough and deeply enough, and you will find that they consider some things are really right and some things are *really* wrong. Without absolutes, morals as morals cease to exist, and humanistic man starting from himself is unable to find the absolute he needs. But because the God of the Bible is there, real morals exist. Within this framework I can say one action is right and another wrong, without talking nonsense.

Fourth, there is an adequate reason for fighting wrong. The Christian never faces the dilemma posed in Camus' book *La Peste*. It simply is not true that he either has to side with the doctor against God by fighting the plague, or join with the priest on God's side and thus be much less than human by not fighting the plague.[1] If this were an *either-or* choice in life, it would indeed be terrible.[2] But the Christian is not confined to such a choice. Let us go to the tomb of Lazarus. As Jesus stood there, he not only wept, but he was *angry*. The exegesis of the Greek of the passages John 11:33 and 38 is clear.[3] Jesus, standing in front of the tomb of Lazarus, was *angry* at death and at the abnormality of the world—the destruction and distress caused by sin. In Camus' words, Christ hated the plague. He claimed to be God, and *he could hate the plague without hating himself as God.*

A Christian can fight what is wrong in the world with compassion and know that as he hates these things, God hates them too. God hates them to the high price of the death of Christ.

But if I live in a world of nonabsolutes and would fight social injustice on the mood of the moment, how can I establish what social justice is? What criterion do I have to distinguish between right and wrong so that I can know what I should be fighting? Is it not possible that I could in fact acquiesce in evil and stamp out good? The word *love* cannot tell me how to discern, for within the humanistic framework love can have no defined meaning. But once I comprehend that the Christ who came to die to end "the plague" both wept and was angry at the plague's effects, I have a reason for fighting that does not rest merely on my momentary disposition, or the shifting consensus of men.

But the Christian also needs to be challenged at this point. The fact that he alone has a sufficient standard by which to fight evil, does not mean that he *will* so fight. The Christian is the real radical of our generation, for he stands against the monolithic, modern concept of truth as relative. But too often, instead of being the radical, standing against the shifting sands of relativism, he subsides into merely maintaining the *status quo.* If it is true that evil is evil, that God hates it to the point of the cross, and that there is a moral law fixed in what God is in himself, then Christians should be the first into the field against what is wrong—including man's inhumanity to man.

5
How Do
We Know
It Is True?

*T*hose interested in my thoughts concerning "apologetics" will find these in appendix A of this book.

All men on their own level face a problem. Confronted with the existence and form of the external universe and the "mannishness" of man, how does it fit together, and what sense does it make?

Imagine a book which has been mutilated, leaving just one inch of printed matter on each page. Although it would obviously be impossible to piece together and understand the book's story, yet few people would imagine that what was left had come together by chance. However, if the torn-off parts of each page were found in the attic and were added in the right places, then the story could be read and would make sense. The whole man would be relieved that the mystery of the book had been solved, and the whole man would be involved in the reading of the completed story; but man's reason would have been the first to tell him that the portions which were discovered were the proper solution to the problem of the ripped book.

Notice two things about this illustration. First, the portions of each page left in the book could never tell what the story was about. Their importance would be as a test to determine whether the pieces found in the attic were the right ones for that book. Second, the man who discovered the matching portions used his reason to show that they fitted the mutilated book. But then, on the level of his whole personality, he enjoyed reading and understanding the complete story of the original pieces and the added portions. This would particularly be the case if the *total* book opened the way to a restored communication with someone important to the reader.

So it is with Christianity: the ripped pages remaining in the book correspond to the abnormal universe and the abnormal man we now have. The parts of the pages which are discovered correspond to the Scriptures which are God's propositional communication to mankind, which not only touch "religious" truth but also the cosmos and history, which are open to verification. Neither the abnormal external world nor the abnormal "mannishness" of man can give the answer to the whole meaning of the created order; yet they are both important in knowing that the Scriptures, God's communication to man, are what they claim to be. The question is whether the communication given by God completes and explains the portions we had before and especially whether it explains what was obvious before, though without an explanation—that is, that the universe exists and the universe and the "mannishness" of man are not just a chance configuration of the printer's scrambled type. To put it another way, does the Bible's answer or does John Cage's chance music speak of what exists?

Rationalistically and autonomously man could not give a proper answer on the basis of the portion of the book that remained. Without the pages which were discovered, man would never have had the answer. Neither do we have a leap of faith, because the pieces match up in a coherent whole over the whole unified field of knowledge. With the propositional communication from the personal God before us not only the things of the cosmos and history match up but everything on the upper and lower stories matches too: grace and nature; a moral absolute and morals; the universal point of reference and the particulars; and the emotional and aesthetic realities of man as well.

Of course, the individual man will not see that they match up if he rejects the communication just because he has not thought it up himself. This would be much the same as the man in our illustration rejecting the pieces of the book found in the attic because he wanted to make up his own story.

The Nature of Proof

In dealing with the question of proof which has been raised by the illustration of the book, I want to suggest that scientific proof, philosophical proof and religious proof follow the same rules. We may have any problem before us which we wish to solve; it may concern a chemical reaction or the meaning of man. After the question has been defined, in each case proof consists of two steps:

A. The theory must be noncontradictory and must give an answer to the phenomenon in question.

B. We must be able to live consistently with our theory. For example, the answer given to the chemical reaction must conform to what we observe in the test tube. With regard to man and his "mannishness," the answer given must conform to what we observe in a wide consideration of man and how he behaves.

Specifically in relation to the question of man, does the Christian answer conform to and explain what we observe concerning man as he is (including my knowledge of myself as a man)? The Christian answer is that man is not dead; rather, that he was man and personal intrinsically from the time he was made by a personal source; and though at the beginning he was normal, he is now abnormal. The reader may well recall here the illustration of the water rising in the second valley and the material in the previous chapters which dealt with the personal source and with man's present abnormality.

Then there is the negative consideration. After a careful definition has weeded out the trivial, the other possible answers that do not involve a mystical leap of faith are of the following nature:

1. That the impersonal plus time plus chance have produced a personal man. But this theory is against all experience and thus usually the advocates of this theory end with a leap of faith, often hidden by the use of connotation words.

2. That man is not personal, but dead; that he is in reality a machine,

and therefore personality is an illusion. This theory could fit the first criterion of being noncontradictory, but it will not fit the second, for man simply cannot live as though he were a machine. This may be observed as far back in the history of man as we have evidence—for example, from the art and artifacts of the caves or from man's burial rites. We have already given many examples of the way in which a man, such as a scientist in love, has been driven to a Jekyll and Hyde existence on the basis of this conclusion. He is one thing in his laboratory, but something completely different at home with his wife and children. Included is the whole struggle of modern man, the despair shown by the acceptance of the irrational leap in a desperate attempt to have answers at the expense of reason, and the scream of the modern artists when they do not find a meaning for man. Although man may say that he is no more than a machine, his whole life denies it.

3. That in the future man will find another reasonable answer. There are, however, two overwhelming problems to this answer. First, this could be said about any answer to anything and would bring all thought and science to an end. It must be seen to be an evasion and an especially weak reply if the person using it applies it only to this one question. Second, no one can live with this answer, for it simply is not possible to hold one's breath and wait until some solution is found in the future. Continually the individual makes moral judgments which affect himself and others, and he must be using some working hypothesis from which to start. Thus, if a person offers this seriously as an alternative theory, he should be prepared to go into deep freeze and stop making judgments which touch on the problem of man. Bertrand Russell, for example, should have stopped making sociological decisions which involved others. This position is only possible if one stops the clock.

4. That the scientific theory of relativity may in the future prove to be a sufficient answer for human life. But the scientific theory of relativity cannot be applied to human life in this way. The scientific theory is constantly being tested, both as a theory and by measurement. Therefore it does not mean that "anything goes," as it does when

relativity is applied to human values. Moreover, in science the speed of light in a vacuum is considered an absolute standard. Therefore, scientific relativity does not imply that all scientific laws are in a constant state of flux. To use scientific relativity to buttress the concept of relativity in regard to human life and human values is completely invalid.

One might think of a few other attempts to find possible answers, but the possibilities are very few indeed.

In contrast to such answers, if the scope of the phenomena under consideration is large enough (that is, if it includes the existence of the universe and its form,[1] and the "mannishness" of man as he now is), Christianity, which begins with the existence of the infinite-personal God, man's creation in his image, and a space-time Fall, does offer a nonself-contradictory answer which explains the phenomena and which can be lived with, both in life and in scholarly pursuits.

I suggest that a serious question has to be faced as to whether the reason why modern men reject the Christian answer, or why they often do not even consider it, is *because they have already accepted, with an implicit faith, the presupposition of the uniformity of natural causes in a closed system.*

This does not mean that the Christian answer should be accepted for pragmatic reasons, but it does mean that the solution given in the Bible answers the problem of the universe and man, and nothing else does.

It should be added in conclusion that the Christian, after he becomes a Christian, has years of experimental evidence to add to all the above reasons. But we may stop at the same place as Paul does in Romans, chapter 1, by saying that the existence of the external universe and its form and the "mannishness" of man demonstrate the truth of the historic Christian position. He does not in Romans 1 go on to appeal to the Christian's experience. "For the wrath of God is revealed from heaven against all ungodliness and unrighteousness of men, who hold down the truth in unrighteousness; because that which may be known of God is manifest in them [the "mannishness" of man], for God manifested it unto them. For the invisible things of him since the creation of the world are clearly seen, being perceived through the things that are made [the external world and its form], even his everlasting power and divinity, that they may be without excuse. "[2]

True Rationality but Not Only Rationality

Although rationality is important, it should never become exclusively so.[3] Rationality is not the end of the matter.[4] It is parallel to the problem of form and freedom in art. The artist, to be an artist, needs to be free. On the other hand, if there is no form to his painting, the artist loses all communication with the viewers. The form makes it possible for the artist to have freedom plus communication. In the same way, rationality is needed to open the door to a vital relationship to God.

The study of verbalized and nonverbalized communication enters here. What form is to the artist, words are to general communication. The use of words, clearly defined and dealt with rationally, gives form and certainty in communication. The same is true with carefully defined scientific symbols.

It is possible to add things to rational verbalization and thus to enrich it. For example, poetry undoubtedly adds something to prose form. In the Psalms something is communicated to us which would not be so in a bare prose account. The same thing is true when the artist paints a portrait. However, if there is an absolute divorce between the defined and rationally comprehended verbalization on one hand and (for example) *bare poetic form* on the other, no certain communication comes across to the reader. The most the reader can do is to use the bare poetic form as a quarry out of which to create something by his own emotions.

As long as a genuine continuity remains between the defined verbalization and what is added, then all kinds of enrichment can be brought in. But if there is discontinuity, then no one can say for certain what the added things mean. This is true in art, in experience and even in the use of figures of speech. Figures of speech enhance communication, so long as they fit into a framework of defined speech which can be rationally considered. But if someone writes a book or a play composed only of figures of speech without any relation to a defined rational context, not only is communication lost but the purpose of the figure of speech itself (to be enriching) is lost.

Therefore it is not that rationality is exclusively important, but rather that rationality defines and provides a form for the whole. In the Scriptures there is a good example of this when John lays down as the only true test of the spirits and prophets something which has content and is rationally based: "Beloved, believe not every spirit, but prove the spirits, whether they are of God: because many false prophets are gone out into the world. Hereby know ye the Spirit of God: every spirit which confesseth that Jesus Christ is come in the flesh is of God: and every spirit that confesseth not Jesus is not of God: and this is the spirit of the antichrist."[5]

The Christian is not rationalistic; he does not try to begin from himself autonomously and work out a system from there on. But he *is* rational: he thinks and acts on the basis that A is A and A is not non-A. However, he does not end with only rationality, for in his response to what God has said his whole personality is involved. Yet, if the control of defined verbalization is lost, then he loses his way. There is no longer any means of testing the spirits, the prophets or experience. All of this then becomes merely the Greek "shade" in the upper story of the new theology to which we referred earlier.

It is therefore most important to get the balance between, on the one hand, the truly rational and, on the other, the involvement of the whole man at every level of his being as something which flows on from the first. Much can be added to the rational, but if we give up the rational everything is lost.

It will help us to clarify this if we go back to the earlier illustration of the ripped book. It is man's reason which is involved in knowing that the communication is the truth of what is; but then, it is the whole man who rejoices in the finding of the missing answer and in the reading of the now *combined* pieces. These combined pieces give knowledge of the infinite-personal God who is there and show how communication with Him may be restored. Reason began the process, and from then on the whole man was involved.

A number of years ago I was at a discussion group in Detroit. An older black pastor was there. We discussed many intellectual and cultural problems and the answers given by Christianity. One would have called the discussion "intellectual" rather than devotional. As he was leaving, the black pastor shook my hand and thanked me. If he had said, "Thank you for helping me to defend my people better," or "Thank you for helping me to be a better evangelist," I would have been very glad that what I had said had been helpful, and then possibly I would not have given it another thought. But what he actually said was, "Thank you for opening these doors to me; now I can worship God better." I will never forget him because he was a man who really understood. If this is not our own response first of all, and then the response of those whom we try to help, we have made a mistake somewhere.

Section Four

Speaking Historic Christianity into the Twentieth-Century Climate

1
Finding the
Point of Tension

Communicating to One of My Kind
Communication means that an idea which I have in my mind passes
through my lips (or fingers—in most art forms) and reaches the other
person's mind. Adequate communication means that when it reaches
the recipient's mind, it is substantially the same as when it left mine.
This does not mean that it will be completely the same, but that he
will nevertheless have substantially realized the point I wish to convey.
The words that we use are only a tool for translating the ideas which
we wish to communicate; we are not trying to convey merely a
succession of verbal sounds.

Because we must use words in order to communicate ideas, there
may be several language problems. The most obvious one arises
between different language groups. If we want to speak to a man, we
must first learn his language.

Another problem is that of time. In the course of history language
changes in meaning; words may not have the same meaning today as
they did in an earlier age. Language naturally changes its meaning as
time passes, and this is uniquely true today with the great differences
above and below the line of despair.

A further language barrier comes as we try to talk to people of a very different social background from ourselves, for example, those in the deep slums.

In none of these cases do the language problems solve themselves automatically. If we wish to communicate, then we must take time and trouble to learn our hearers' use of language so that they understand what we intend to convey. This is particularly difficult today for us as Christians when we want to use a word like *God* or *guilt* in a strictly defined sense rather than as a connotation word, because the concepts of these words have been changed universally. In a case like this, either we must try to find a synonymous word without a false connotation, or else we have to define the word at length when we use it, so that we make sure our hearer understands as fully as possible what we are conveying. In this latter case we are no longer using the word as a technical word, in the sense that we assume a common definition.

I suggest that if the word (or phrase) we are in the habit of using is no more than an orthodox evangelical cliché which has become a technical term among Christians, then we should be willing to give it up when we step outside our own narrow circle and talk to the people around us. If, on the other hand, the word is indispensable, such as the word *God,* then we should talk at sufficient length to make ourselves clear. Technical words, if they are used without sufficient explanation, may mean that outsiders really do not hear the Christian message at all and that we ourselves, in our churches and missions, have become an introverted and isolated language group.

As we turn to consider in more detail how we may speak to people of the twentieth century, we must emphasize first of all that we cannot apply mechanical rules. We, of all people, should realize this, for as Christians we believe that personality really does exist and is important. We can lay down some general principles, but there can be no automatic application. If we are truly personal, as created by God, then each individual will differ from everyone else. Therefore each person must be dealt with as an individual, not as a case or statistic or machine. If we would work with these people, we cannot apply the things we have dealt with in this book mechanically. We must look to the Lord in prayer, and to the work of the Holy Spirit, for the effective use of these things.

Furthermore, we must remember that the person to whom we are talking, however far from the Christian faith he may be, is an image-bearer of God. He has great value, and our communication to him must be in genuine love. Love is not an easy thing; it is not just an emotional urge but an attempt to move over and sit in the other person's place and see how his problems look to him. Love is a genuine concern for the individual. As Jesus Christ reminds us, we are to love that individual "as ourselves." This is the place to begin. Therefore, to be engaged in personal "witness" as a duty or because our Christian circle exerts a social pressure on us is to miss the whole point. The reason we do it is that the person before us is an image-bearer of God, and he is an individual who is unique in the world. This kind of communication is not cheap. To understand and speak to sincere but utterly confused twentieth-century people is costly. It is tiring; it will open you to temptations and pressures. Genuine love, in the last analysis, means a willingness to be entirely exposed to the person to whom we are talking.

The one before us is our kind. The Bible teaches that there are two humanities; yet looking at it another way, there is only one humanity. There are two humanities in the sense that there are those still in rebellion against God, and there are those who have returned to God through Jesus Christ. But this should not dull us to the fact that God "hath made of one blood all nations of men for to dwell on all the face of the earth."[1] This does not just mean that the whole human race is biologically one, in the sense that we can reproduce together, but that we are all descended from Adam as a common ancestor. Thus, emotionally as well as intellectually, we must look at the man before us as *our kind*. This man is our counterpart; he is lost, but so once were we. We are one flesh, one blood, one kind.

Finally, as we consider how we are to communicate to man, we must bear in mind that we are speaking to him as a unit. We are not merely dealing with just one part of him called the "soul" in an attempt to get that to heaven. We are conscious that the Bible teaches the unity of the personality. So as we try to communicate in this wholeness this must be reflected in our attitude, as well as in what we say.

Logical Conclusions

We can look now at some of the general principles to guide our communication with twentieth-century man.

Let us remember that every person we speak to, whether shop girl or university student, has a set of presuppositions, whether he or she has analyzed them or not. The dot in the diagram represents a person's non-Christian presuppositions; the arrow points to what would be the logical conclusion of those non-Christian presuppositions.

A man with his non-
Christian presuppositions   •——————— ⟹ | The logical conclusion of his non-
Christian presuppositions

If a man were completely logical to his presuppositions, he would come out at the line on the right. If he arrived there in thinking and life, he would be consistent to his presuppositions.

But, in fact, no non-Christian can be consistent to the logic of his presuppositions. The reason for this is simply that a man must live in reality, and reality consists of two parts: the external world and its form, and man's "mannishness," including his own "mannishness." No matter what a man may believe, he cannot change the reality of what is. As Christianity is the truth of what is there, to deny this, on the basis of another system, is to stray from the real world:

The real world— | The logical conclusion of a man's non-
the external world   ⟸ ——————— ⟹ | Christian presuppositions
and man himself |

Every man, therefore, irrespective of his system, is caught. As he tries intellectually to extend his position in a logical way and then live within it, he is caught by the two things which, as it were, slap him across the face. Without indicating that his psychology or philosophy is correct, Carl Gustav Jung has correctly observed that two things cut across every man's will—the external world with its structure, and those things which well up from inside himself. Non-Christian presuppositions simply do not fit into what God has made, including what man is. This being so, every man is in a place of tension. Man cannot make his own universe and then live in it.

The Bible takes this point a step further when it says that, even in hell, a man cannot be consistent to his non-Christian presuppositions: "If I make my bed in hell, behold, thou [God] art there."[2] Man will be separated from communion with God in hell, but no one is going to be able to form hell to make their own universe in a limited area. Man there will still be in the universe of God. Hence, even in hell, a man cannot be consistent to his non-Christian presuppositions.

In this present life it is the same. It is impossible for any non-Christian individual or group to be consistent to their system in logic or in practice. Thus, when you face twentieth-century man, whether he is brilliant or an ordinary man of the street, a man of the university or the docks, you are facing a man in tension; and it is this tension which works on your behalf as you speak to him. If I did not know this from the Word of God and personal experience, I would not have the courage to step into the circles I do. A man may try to bury the tension and you may have to help him find it, but somewhere there is a point of inconsistency. He stands in a position which he cannot pursue to the end; and this is not just an intellectual concept of tension, it is what is wrapped up in what he is as a man.

Torn by Two Consistencies

Christian apologetics do not start somewhere beyond the stars. They begin with man and what he knows about himself. When a man is lost, he is lost against all that there is, including what he is. Therefore, when he stands before God in judgment, God, in order to point out how false his position has been, will only need to refer to what he as an individual has known of the external world and "mannishness." As far as morals are concerned, man will only have to be judged according to the standards he himself has laid down in condemning others, for, as Paul makes clear, he then proceeds deliberately to break even his own standards.[3]

Hence, the person before you is not in a vacuum. He knows something of the external world, and he knows something of himself.

Every person is somewhere along the line between the real world and the logical conclusion of his or her non-Christian presuppositions.

Every person has the pull of two consistencies, the pull towards the real world and the pull towards the logic of his system. He may let the pendulum swing back and forth between them, but he cannot live in both places at once. He will be living nearer to the one or to the other, depending on the strength of the pull at any given time. To have to choose between one consistency or the other is a real damnation for man. *The more logical a man who holds a non-Christian position is to his own presuppositions, the further he is from the real world; and the nearer he is to the real world, the more illogical he is to his presuppositions.*

The Tensions Are Felt in Differing Strengths

We have said that every person, however intelligent or lacking in intelligence, has stopped somewhere along the line towards the consistent conclusion of his own position. Some people are prepared to go further from the real world than others in an attempt to be more logical to their presuppositions. The French existentialists Camus and Sartre exhibited this:

Sartre said that Camus was not sufficiently consistent on the basis of their mutual presuppositions. The reason for this was because Camus never gave up "hope," centered in random personal happiness, though it went against the logic of his position. Or as was stated when Camus received the Nobel prize, because he never gave up the search for morals, though the world seemed to be without meaning. These are the reasons why, of the two, Camus was more loved in the intellectual world. He never got the real world sorted out, as we have seen from his book *The Plague*, but he was nearer to it than Sartre.

Sartre was correct to say that Camus was illogical to their presuppositions; but as we saw before, he could not be consistent either. When he signed the Algerian Manifesto, taking a position as though morals have real meaning, he too was being inconsistent to his presuppositions. Thus Sartre was also in tension.

Each person may move up or down the line at different times in their lives, according to their circumstances, but most people more or less stabilize at one point. Every non-Christian, whether he is sleeping under the bridges in Paris or is totally bourgeois, is somewhere along the line.

The real world—
the external world
and man himself

The logical conclusion of
a man's non-Christian
presuppositions

This is not an abstraction, for each of these persons is created in the image of God, and thus is in tension because within himself there are things which speak of the real world. Men in different cultures have different standards for morals, but there is no one who does not have some moral motions. Follow a modern girl through her day. She may seem totally amoral. But if you were to get to know her you would find that, at some point, she felt the pull of morals. Love may carry different expressions, but all men have some motions of love. The individual will feel this tension in different ways—with some it will be beauty, with some it will be significance, with some it will be rationality, with some it will be the fear of nonbeing.

Man today seeks to deflect this tension by saying that he is no more than a machine. But if he were no more than a machine, he would find no difficulty in proceeding step by step down the line to the logical conclusion of his non-Christian presuppositions. Man is not a machine, however, even if he says he is.

Suppose that a satellite were put into orbit around the earth with a camera that was able to photograph everything on the world's surface. If this information was then fed back to a giant computer that did not need programming, it might calculate that everything behaved mechanically. But the final observer is not a computer but the individual man. There is always one person in the room who does not allow everything to be seen as machinelike; it is myself, the observer, because I know myself.

Christians must be careful at this place. Though the Bible says men are lost, it does not say they are nothing. When a man says he is a machine or nothing, he makes himself less than the Bible's view of fallen man.

Therefore, the first consideration in our apologetics for modern man, whether factory-hand or research student, is to find the place where his tension exists. We will not always find it easy to do this. Many people have never analyzed their own point of tension. Since the Fall man is separated from himself. Man is complicated, and he tries to bury himself in himself. Therefore, it will take time and it will cost something to discover what the person we are speaking to often has not yet discovered for himself. Down inside of himself man finds it easy to lie to himself. We, in love, looking to the work of the Holy Spirit, must reach down into that person and try to find where the point of tension is.

2
From the Point of Tension to the Gospel

Why There Is a Place for Conversation

If the man before you were logical to his non-Christian presuppositions, you would have no point of communication with him. It would be impossible to have communication if he were consistent.[1] But in reality no one can live logically according to his own non-Christian presuppositions, and consequently, because he is faced with the real world and himself, in *practice* you will find a place where you can talk. He would not be where he is, suspended between the real world and the logical conclusions of his presuppositions, if he were consistent. The only reason he can be at the point of tension, nearer to the real world than his presuppositions would logically indicate, is because, to some extent, he is not logical; and the nearer he is to the real world, the more illogical he is to his presuppositions. As an illustration: it is illogical for John Cage to pick mushrooms as he does, in a universe which, he says, is intrinsically chance, but, illogically, he does pick them in that way; and thus you could start talking to him concerning the inadequacy of his system, with its chance music, in relationship to his mushrooms.

In *practice* then, we do have a point for conversation, but this point is not properly to be spoken of as "neutral." There are no neutral facts, for facts are God's facts. However, there is common ground between the Christian and non-Christian because regardless of a man's system, he has to live in God's world. If he were consistent to his non-Christian presuppositions, he would be separated from the real universe and the real man, and conversation and communication would not be possible.[2]

In this way it does not seem to me that presuppositional apologetics should be seen as ending conversation with the people around us. On the other hand, to try to work below the line of despair without a clear and defined concept of presuppositional apologetics is simply to destroy the possibility of helping twentieth-century people. There is no use talking today until the presuppositions are taken into account, and especially the crucial presuppositions concerning the nature of truth and the method of attaining truth.

Giving and Taking Blows

When we have discovered, as well as we can, a person's point of tension, the next step is to push him towards the logical conclusion of his presuppositions:

The real world—
the external world
and man himself

The logical conclusion of
a man's non-Christian
presuppositions

We ought not to try first to move a man away from the logical conclusion of his position but towards it, in the direction of the arrow. We should try to move him in the natural direction his presuppositions take him. We are pushing him towards the place where he ought to be, had he not stopped short.

As I seek to do this, I need to remind myself constantly that this is not a game I am playing. If I begin to enjoy it as a kind of intellectual exercise, then I am cruel and can expect no real spiritual results. As I push the man off his false balance, he must be able to feel that I care for him. Otherwise I will only end up destroying him, and the cruelty and ugliness of it all will destroy me as well. Merely to be abstract and cold is to show that I do not really believe this person to be created in God's image and therefore one of my kind. Pushing him towards the logic of his presuppositions is going to cause him pain; therefore, I must not push any further than I need to.

If we find the man ready to receive Christ as Savior, then by all means we should not talk about presuppositions but tell him the glorious good news. The whole purpose of our speaking to twentieth-century people in the way I have outlined is not to make them admit that we are right in some personally superior way, nor to push their noses in the dirt, but to make them see their need so that they will listen to the gospel. As soon as the person before us is ready to listen to the gospel, we do not push him any further—it is horrible to be propelled in the direction of meaninglessness, against the testimony of the external world and the testimony of oneself.

As we get ready to tell the person God's answer to his or her need, we must make sure that the individual understands that we are talking about real *truth*, and not about something vaguely religious which seems to work psychologically. We must make sure that he understands that we are talking about *real guilt* before God, and we are not offering him merely relief for his guilt-feelings. We must make sure that he understands that we are talking to him about *history*, and that the death of Jesus was not just an ideal or a symbol but a fact of space and time. If we are talking to a person who would not understand the term "space-time history," we can ask: "Do you believe that Jesus died in the sense that if you had been there that day, you could have rubbed your finger on the cross and got a splinter in it?" *Until he understands the importance of these three things, he is not ready to become a Christian.*

Push him towards the logic of his position in the area of his own real interests. If he is interested in science, we will push him to the logical conclusion of his position in science. If it is art, then gently and yet firmly we push him from the point of tension to the end of his presuppositions. At all points in the conversation, we must allow him to ask any question he wants. We cannot say, on the one hand, that we believe in the unity of truth and then, on the other hand, suddenly withdraw from the discussion and tell him to believe on blind authority. He has a right to ask questions. It is perfectly true that not all Christians proceed in this way with all modern people, and yet people are brought to Christ by them. For every person who is saved we should be very thankful. But to withdraw by saying or implying "Keep quiet and just believe" may later lead to spiritual weakness, even if the person does become a Christian, for it will leave crucial questions unanswered. Therefore, in the midst of our attempts to press our case, we must be ready to receive blows as well. The more he is a true twentieth-century man the more important it is, if you wish to see him become a Christian, that you should accept the blows of the questions in the name of Jesus Christ, and in the name of truth. On the other hand, keep pressing him back, for *he* must keep answering questions too. As we take time to study both the modern world in which we live and, more particularly, our Bible, we shall come to know more and more answers. We must have faced the question "Is Christianity true?" for ourselves. We must be men of the Scriptures, so that we can know what the content of the biblical system is. Every day of our lives we should be studying the Scriptures to make sure that what we are presenting really is the Christian position, and that we are presenting it as well as possible in our day.

Taking the Roof Off

Let us think of it in a slightly different way. Every man has built a roof over his head to shield himself at the point of tension:

The real world—
the external world
and man himself

The logical conclusion of
a man's non-Christian
presuppositions

At the point of tension the person is not in a place of consistency in his system, and the roof is built *as a protection against the blows of the real world,* both internal and external. It is like the great shelters built upon some mountain passes to protect vehicles from the avalanches of rock and stone which periodically tumble down the mountain. The avalanche, in the case of the non-Christian, is the real but abnormal, fallen world which surrounds him. The Christian, lovingly, must remove the shelter and allow the truth of the external world and of what man is to beat upon him. When the roof is off, each man must stand naked and wounded before the truth of what is.

The truth that we let in first is not a dogmatic statement of the truth of the Scriptures, but the truth of the external world and the truth of what man himself is. This is what shows him his need. The Scriptures then show him the real nature of his lostness and the answer to it. *This, I am convinced, is the true order for our apologetics in the second half of the twentieth century for people living under the line of despair.*

| The real world—
the external world
and man himself | | The logical conclusion of
a man's non-Christian
presuppositions |

It is unpleasant to be submerged by an avalanche, but we must allow the person to undergo this experience so that he may realize his system has no answer to the crucial questions of life. He must come to know that his roof is a false protection from the storm of what is, and then we can talk to him of the storm of the judgment of God.

Removing the roof is not some kind of optional exercise. It is strictly biblical in its emphasis. In the thinking of the twentieth-century man, the concept of judgment and of hell is nonsense, and therefore to begin to talk here is to mumble in a language which makes no contact with him. Hell or any such concept is unthinkable to modern man because he has been brainwashed into accepting the monolithic belief of naturalism which surrounds him. We of the West may not be brainwashed by our State, but we are brainwashed by our culture. Even the modern radicals are radicals in a very limited circle.

Before men passed below the line of despair they knew for the most part that they were guilty, but it rarely entered their minds that they were dead as well. By contrast, modern man hardly ever considers himself to be guilty, but he often acknowledges that he is dead. The Bible says that both these things are true. Man in revolt against the holy God who is there is guilty and is already under God's wrath. Because he is guilty, he is separated from his true and only reference point and therefore he is dead as well. The Bible does not say man will become lost, but that he *is* lost. The chasm in biblical teaching does not come at death but at the point of conversion, when the individual passes from death to life. This is the point of personal antithesis; before that, man is dead indeed.

Hence we begin to deal with "modern man" by preaching at the place where he can understand. Often he understands the horrible point of meaninglessness. Often he recognizes the tension between the real world and the logic of his presuppositions. Often he appreciates the horror of being dead and yet still alive. The Word of God is overwhelmingly clear in its teaching that there are two aspects of lostness: present and future. When I accept Christ as Savior, I pass from death to life, *and therefore before that time I am clearly dead.* Therefore, when modern man feels dead, he is experiencing what the Word of God tells him he is. In himself he will not be able to define his deadness, for he does not know what his deadness is—and even less does he know the solution to it. However, he is aware of one thing, and that is that he is dead. It is our task to tell him that the present death he knows is moral death and not just metaphysical lostness, and then to tell him God's solution. But we begin with the present lostness with which he wrestles. This is not adding to the gospel; it is applying in practice the depths of the truth of the Word of God, that man in revolt is purposeless and dead.

This is what we mean by taking the roof off. But we cannot ever think this to be easy. The hardest thing of all is that when we have exposed modern man to his tension, he still may not be willing for the true solution. Consequently, we may seem to leave him in a worse state than he was in before. But this is the same as the evangelism of the past. Whenever the evangelist preached the reality of hell, men who did not believe were more miserable after hearing his preaching than if they had never heard him. We are in the same position. We confront men with reality; we remove their protection and their escapes; we allow the avalanches to fall. If they do not become Christians, then indeed they are in a worse state than before we spoke to them.

3
Applying the Gospel

How Dare We Do It?

How dare we deal with men in this way? Only for one reason—because Christianity is truth. If we are *not* functioning in the area that this is absolute truth, such evangelism is cruel beyond measure. But if this is truth, if it is true that this man before me is separated from God and lost now and for eternity, then even though in individual cases men do not accept Christ and are left worse off than when I began, I must nevertheless have the courage so to speak. If there is a thesis, there is an antithesis. If there is that which is true truth, there is that which is error. If there is true Christian salvation (in contrast to the concept of salvation in the new theology), there is lostness.

When I began to approach individuals in this way, some years ago now, my wife said to me, "Are you not afraid that someone will commit suicide one day?" Since then we have had one girl who tried to do this; fortunately she did not die and later on made a profession of faith. But even if she had succeeded, after walking in the mountains and crying before God, I would have begun the same way with the next person who came.

We cannot do this until we have personally faced the question as to whether the Judeo-Christian system is true in the way we have been speaking of truth. When we are certain about this for ourselves, then if we love men we shall have the courage to lift the roof off other people's lives and expose them to the collapse of their defenses. We ourselves, as we face these people, must have the integrity to continue to live open to the questions: Does God exist? Is the content of the Judeo-Christian system truth?

The more comprehending we are as we take the roof off, the worse the man will feel if he rejects the Christian answer. In a fallen world we must be willing to face the fact that however lovingly we preach the gospel, if a man rejects it he will be miserable. It is dark out there. I think one reason I am able to talk to this kind of twentieth-century person is because I understand something of just how dark it can be. Men must know that with integrity we have faced the reality of the dark path they are treading.

Once at Cambridge University a postgraduate student said to me, in front of a group that had gathered in his room, "Mr. Schaeffer, I heard you speak last year. Since then I have been preparing a paper and I would like to read it to you. I dare read it to you because I think you understand. Sir, I am in horror of great darkness." There is no romanticism as one seeks to move a man in the direction of honesty. On the basis of his system you are pushing him further and further towards that which is not only totally against God, but also against himself. You are pushing him out of the real universe. Of course it hurts; of course it is dark in the place where a man, in order to be consistent to his non-Christian presuppositions, must deny what is there in this life as well as in the next.

Often it takes much more time to press him towards the logical conclusion of his position than it does later take to give him the answer. Luther spoke of the Law and the Gospel; and the Law, the need, must always be adequately clear first. Then one can give the Christian answer because he knows his need for something; and one can tell him what his deadness really is, and the solution in the total structure of truth. But if we do not take sufficient time to take the roof off, the twentieth-century man will not comprehend what we are trying to communicate, either what his death is caused by, or the solution. We must never forget that the first part of the gospel is not "Accept Christ as Savior" but "God is there." Only then are we ready to hear God's solution for man's *moral* dilemma in the substitutionary work of Christ in history.

When we have reached this point with a man, we discover that however complicated the modern man may be under the line of despair, however sophisticated or cultured or filled with knowledge, when he sees his need the good news is the same as it has always been. The wonderful thing is that at this point not only can the same ideas be given but even the same words used to all men.

I recall a time some years ago when two people professed belief in Christ on the same day. One was a very intelligent doctor and the other a very simple Swiss peasant. In my previous conversations with them, the peasant would have understood little of my talks with the doctor. Yet on this day, when both of them had come to understand their need, as I spoke first to one and then to the other, I was able to use not only the same ideas but exactly the same words in telling each one the answer to the need. There is no point in being complicated once the intelligent or the simple man understands his need; the same ideas and even the same words are all that is needed.

The problem which confronts us as we approach modern man today is *not* how we are to change Christian teaching in order to make it more palatable, for to do that would mean throwing away any chance of giving the real answer to man in despair; rather, it is the problem of how to communicate the gospel so that it is understood.

Faith in the Biblical Sense

In the first place, Christian faith turns on the reality of God's existence, his being there.[1] Then it also turns on an acceptance of the fact that man's dilemma is moral and not metaphysical. Each person must face these two things on his own level as a matter of truth.

The Philippian jailer asked Paul and Silas, "What must I do to be saved?" The passage which follows is: "Believe on the Lord Jesus, and thou shalt be saved, thou and thy house. And they spake the word of the Lord unto him, with all that were in his house."[2]

What Paul and Silas said in reply to the question was not spoken in a vacuum. Because of the earthquake and the remarkable way Paul and Silas behaved in prison, the jailer had reason to be aware of the existence of a personal God—one who acts in history, answers prayers, and gives men reality in their lives. But this was not all. The whole city had been in an uproar because of all that Paul and Silas had been saying and doing *before* they were put into prison. Finally, it seems from the preciseness of the jailer's question and from what we know elsewhere of Paul's preaching that the jailer had heard the Christian message from Paul himself.

After he had taken them to his house, we read that Paul and Silas spoke to him and his household further of the things of the Lord. Only after this—which we have no reason to think was merely a few minutes' conversation—did they all believe.

True Christian faith rests on content. It is not a vague thing which takes the place of real understanding, nor is it the strength of belief which is of value. *The true basis for faith is not the faith itself but the work which Christ finished on the cross.* My believing is not the basis for being saved—the basis is the work of Christ. Christian faith is turned outward to an objective person: "Believe on the Lord Jesus, and thou shalt be saved."

Once the truth of God's existence is known to us, and we know that we have true moral guilt before a holy God, then we should be glad to know the solution to our dilemma. The solution is from God's side, not ours.

Now the content of God's propositional promises begins to be wonderful to us. Paul and Silas made such a propositional promise to the jailer, and in the Bible God gives such propositional promises more generally. For example, John 3:36 reads: "He that believeth on the Son has everlasting life: and he that believeth not the Son shall not see life, but the wrath of God abideth on him." There is a strong antithesis here. The second part of the verse speaks of man's present and future lostness; the first part of the verse gives God's solution. The call to Christian believing rests on God's propositional promises. We are to consider whether these things are true, but then we are faced with a choice—either we believe him, or we call God a liar and walk away, unwilling to bow to him.

As a man is faced with God's promises, Christian faith means bowing twice: First, he needs to bow in the realm of Being (metaphysically)—that is, to acknowledge that he is a creature before the infinite-personal Creator who is there. Second, he needs to bow in the realm of morals—that is, to acknowledge that he has sinned and therefore that he has true guilt before the God who is there. If he has true moral guilt before an infinite God, he has the problem that he, as finite, has no way to remove such a guilt. Thus what he needs is a nonhumanist solution. Now he is faced with God's propositional promise, "Believe on the Lord Jesus, and thou shalt be saved."

What remains is the meaning of "believe on the Lord Jesus." What does it mean to believe on, to cast oneself on, Christ? I would suggest there are four crucial aspects. More detail could be considered, but these are crucial. They are not slogans to be repeated by rote and they do not have to be said in these words, but the individual must have come to a positive conclusion and affirmation concerning them, if he is to believe in the biblical sense:

1. Do you believe that God exists and that he is a personal God, and that Jesus Christ is God—remembering that we are not talking of the *word* or *idea* god, but of the infinite-personal God who is there?

2. Do you acknowledge that you are guilty in the presence of this God—remembering that we are not talking about guilt-feelings but true moral guilt?

3. Do you believe that Jesus Christ died in space and time, in history, on the cross, and that when he died his substitutional work of bearing God's punishment against sin was fully accomplished and complete?

4. On the basis of God's promises in his written communication to us, the Bible, do you (or have you) cast yourself on this Christ as your personal Savior—not trusting in anything you yourself have ever done or ever will do?

But note with care that God's promise, "He that believeth on the Son has everlasting life," rests upon God's being there; Christ being the Second Person of the Trinity, whose death therefore has infinite value; my not coming presumptuously in, thinking I can save myself, but casting myself on the finished work of Christ and the written promises of God. My faith is simply the empty hands by which I accept God's free gift.

John Bunyan in *Pilgrim's Progress* has Hopeful say it this way:
He [Faithful] bid me go to him and see. Then I said it was presumption. He said, no, for I was invited to come.[3] Then he gave me a book of Jesus' inditing, to encourage me the more freely to come; and he said concerning that book, that every jot and tittle thereof stood firmer than heaven and earth. Then I asked him further how I must make my supplication to him; and he said, Go and thou shalt find him upon a mercy-seat, where he sits all year long to give pardon and forgiveness to them that come. I told him that I knew not what to say when I came; and he bid me say to this effect: God be merciful to me a sinner, and make me to know and believe in Jesus Christ; for I see, that if his righteousness had not been, or I have not faith in that righteousness, I am utterly cast away. Lord, I have heard that thou art a merciful God, and hast ordained that thy Son Jesus Christ should be the Saviour of the world; and moreover, that thou art willing to bestow him upon a poor sinner as I am—and I am a sinner indeed. Lord, take therefore this opportunity and magnify thy grace in the salvation of my soul through thy Son Jesus Christ."

Bunyan says that Hopeful did not understand at once, but soon he did and said: "From all which, I gathered that I must look for righteousness in his person, and for satisfaction for my sins by his blood; that what he did in obedience to his Father's law, and in submitting to the penalty thereof, was not for himself but for him that will accept it for his salvation, and be thankful."[4]

This is what "believing on the Lord Jesus" means. If a man has believed in this way, he has God's promise that he is a Christian.[5]

Of course, *becoming* a Christian is just the beginning, but we will think more about that in the last section of this book.

After a person has become a Christian, four things will help him:

1. A regular study of the Bible, which is God's communication to us.

2. Regular prayer. Now that our guilt has been removed, there is no barrier between us and God and we are able to talk freely with him. There are two kinds of praying we shall need to practice: special times of prayer, and the constant looking to the Lord as we go about our daily tasks.

3. Talking to others about the God who exists and his solution to man's dilemma.

4. Regular attendance at a church where the Bible is believed. This does not mean every church, but one that is true to the content of the Bible, and one which does not just recite the right words, but where there is a living of the truth in community and compassion to those in the church and to those outside of it.

Section Five

Pre-evangelism
Is No Soft Option

1

Commending the
Christian Faith
to Our Generation

Defense of the Faith

There are two purposes of Christian apologetics. The first is defense. The second is to communicate Christianity in a way that any given generation can understand.

Defense is proper and necessary because in every age historic Christianity will be under attack. Defense does not mean being on the defensive. One must not be embarrassed about the use of the word *defense*. The proponents of any position who are alive to their own generation must give a sufficient answer for it when questions are raised about it. Thus, the word *defense* is not used here in a negative sense, because in any conversation, in any communication which is really dialogue, answers must be given to objections raised.

Such answers are necessary in the first place for myself as a Christian if I am going to maintain my intellectual integrity, and if I am to keep united my personal, devotional and intellectual life. In the second place, these answers are necessary for the sake of those for whom I have a responsibility.

It is unreasonable to expect people of the next generation in any age to continue in the historic Christian position, unless they are helped to see where arguments and connotations directed against Christianity and against them as Christians, by their generation, are fallacious. We must prepare Christian young people to face the monolithic twentieth-century culture by teaching them what the particular attack in our generation is, in contrast to the attacks of previous generations.

I find that everywhere I go—both in the United States and in other countries—children of Christians are being lost to historic Christianity. This is happening not only in small groups in small geographical areas, but everywhere. They are being lost because their parents are unable to understand their children, and therefore cannot really help them in their time of need. This lack of understanding is not only on the part of individual parents but often also of churches, Christian colleges and Christian missions. Some Christian colleges (and I am not talking of "liberal" colleges) lose many of the best students before they graduate. We have left the next generation naked in the face of the twentieth-century thought by which they are surrounded.

So then, the defense, for myself and for those for whom I am responsible, must be a conscious defense. We cannot assume that because we are Christians in the full biblical sense, and indwelt by the Holy Spirit, automatically we shall be free from the influence of what surrounds us. The Holy Spirit can do what he will, but the Bible does not separate his work from knowledge; nor does the work of the Holy Spirit remove our responsibility as parents, pastors, evangelists, missionaries or teachers.

Communication of the Faith

Having said that, however, Christian apologetics should never be restricted to guarding against attack. We have a responsibility to communicate the gospel to our generation.

Christian apologetics is not like living in a castle with the drawbridge up and occasionally tossing a stone over the walls. It is not to be based on a citadel mentality—sitting inside and saying, "You cannot reach me here." If the Christian adopts this attitude, either in theory or in practice, his contacts with those who have accepted twentieth-century thought will stop. Apologetics should not be merely an academic subject, a new kind of scholasticism. It should be thought out and practiced in the rough and tumble of living contact with the present generation. Thus, the Christian should not be interested only in presenting a nicely balanced system on its own, like some Greek metaphysical system, but rather in something which has constant contact with reality—the reality of the questions being asked by his own and the next generation.

No one can become a Christian unless he understands what Christianity is saying. Many pastors, missionaries and Christian teachers seem to be helpless as they try to speak to the educated people and the mass of people about them. They do not seem to face the fact that it is our task to speak to *our* generation; the past has gone, the future is not yet here. *So the positive side of apologetics is the communication of the gospel to the present generation in terms that they can understand.*

The purpose of "apologetics" is not just to win an argument or a discussion, but that the people with whom we are in contact may become Christians and then live under the lordship of Christ in the whole spectrum of life.

It is important to remember, first of all, that we cannot separate true apologetics from the work of the Holy Spirit, nor from a living relationship in prayer to the Lord on the part of the Christian. We must understand that eventually the battle is not just against flesh and blood.

However, the biblical emphasis that knowledge is needed prior to salvation will influence us in attaining that knowledge which is needed to communicate the gospel. Historic Christianity has never separated itself from knowledge. It insists that all truth is one, and we must live and teach this even if twentieth-century thought and theology deny it.

The invitation to act comes only after an adequate base of knowledge has been given. This accords with the reason John gave for writing his Gospel: "Many other signs therefore did Jesus in the presence of his disciples which are not written in this book. But these are written that ye may believe that Jesus is the Christ, the Son of God: and that believing ye may have life in his name."[1] The word *sign* is related to the historic events of the life, death and resurrection of Christ as put forth in this Gospel. In twentieth-century language we could translate *sign* as "space-time proof": "Many other space-time proofs therefore did Jesus." Note first that these space-time proofs which, by their very nature, are observable were set forth as having taken place in the presence of the disciples who observed them. And not only that, but that they were written down in verbalized form. This means, of course, that these space-time proofs can be considered on the basis of the normal use of language as set forth in grammars and lexicons.

The order in these verses is important. First, these are space-time proofs in written form, and consequently capable of careful consideration. Then, second, these proofs are of such a nature as to give good and sufficient evidence that Christ is the Messiah as prophesied in the Old Testament, and also that he is the Son of God. So that, third, we are not asked to believe until we have faced the question as to whether this is true on the basis of the space-time evidence.

The same kind of groundwork of true knowledge is set forth in the prologue to the Gospel of Luke:[2] "Forasmuch as many have taken in hand to draw up a narrative concerning those matters which have been fulfilled among us" (there are things which have happened in history, in the space-time before "us"), "even as they delivered them unto us, which from the beginning were eyewitnesses" (this history is open to verification by eyewitnesses) "and ministers of the word, it seemed good to me also, having traced the course of all things accurately from the first, to write unto thee in order, most excellent Theophilus" (what is open to verification can also be communicated verbally, in writing) "that thou mightest know the truth concerning the things (or words) wherein thou wast instructed." There is no leap in the dark, for it is possible to "know the truth." Only when we have understood this introduction are we ready for the rest of the Gospel of Luke, beginning in the next verse: "There was in the days of Herod, King of Judaea, a certain priest . . ." We know from the prologue that Luke is dealing with a framework of historic truth, and we are to place Herod, Zacharias and Christ within this space-time framework.

Knowledge precedes faith. This is crucial in understanding the Bible. *To say (as a Christian should) that only that faith which believes God on the basis of knowledge is true faith, is to say something which causes an explosion in the twentieth-century world.*

2
The
Importance
of Truth

Some time ago I was speaking at Oxford University to a group of theological students on the subject of communicating the gospel to those people who are dominated by the consensus of twentieth-century thinking. When I had finished speaking, a Canadian postgraduate student stood up and said, "Sir, if we understand you correctly, you are saying that pre-evangelism must come before evangelism. If this is so, then we have been making a mistake at Oxford. The reason we have not been reaching many of these people is because we have not taken enough time with pre-evangelism." I said that I totally agreed.

Truth Stands Before Conversion
Before a man is ready to become a Christian, he must have a proper understanding of truth, whether he has fully analyzed his concept of truth or not. All people, whether they realize it or not, function in the framework of some concept of truth. Our concept of truth will radically affect our understanding of what it means to become a Christian. We are concerned, at this point, not with the *content* of truth so much as with the *concept* of what truth is.

Some who consider themselves real Christians have been infiltrated by the twentieth-century thought-forms. In reference to conversion, in a Christian sense, truth must be first. The phrase "accepting Christ as Savior" can mean anything. We are not saying what we are trying to say unless we make completely clear that we are talking about objective truth when we say Christianity is true and therefore that "accepting Christ as Savior" is not just some form of "upper-story leap."

Truth and Spirituality

Just as this matter of objective truth needs to be stressed before we can do effective evangelism, so the same thing must be considered before we can talk about true spirituality. From the biblical viewpoint, spirituality is not fragmented. Therefore, it has to be distinguished from modern concepts of spirituality, both in the West and the East, and, unhappily, from some evangelical concepts. It is not fragmented because it concerns the whole man in his whole moment-by-moment life. Over against this true biblical view, some evangelicalism has been Platonic in the sense that it has placed too much emphasis on the soul in contrast to the whole person, including the body and the intellect.

It is very important to realize, over against modern concepts of "spiritual experience," that the biblically based experience rests firmly on truth. It is not only an emotional experience, nor is it contentless.

We can think of true spirituality as having three parts. The indispensable beginning is to consider who (or what) "is there," and how I can have a relationship to him (or it). That something must be understood and defined. You cannot have a personal relationship with something unknown. Then, having understood who it is with whom I am to have a personal relationship and how I may have it, comes the actual step of entering into that relationship. The Bible calls this being converted, "born again," and this is a step which a person can take only as an individual. We cannot be born again in groups, but only one at a time. But to say that this is an individual matter is not the same as to say it is individualistic. The words may sound alike, but they are worlds apart. This gives the basis for a whole sociological and cultural concept.

True spirituality cannot be abstracted from truth at one end, nor from the whole man and the whole culture at the other. If there is a true spirituality, it must encompass all. The Bible insists that truth is one—and it is almost the sole surviving system in our generation that does.

To avoid confusion, let us notice what this emphasis on the unity of truth does *not* involve. First of all, from the biblical viewpoint, truth is not ultimately related to orthodoxy. Orthodoxy is important, and I am known as a man who is a convinced orthodox theologian. But truth is not ultimately related to orthodoxy. Second, truth is not related ultimately to the Creeds either. I also believe the historic Christian Creeds are important, but we must realize that, while the Creeds are important, truth is not finally related to them. Truth is related to something back of both orthodoxy and the Creeds.

Third, truth is not *ultimately* related even to the Scriptures. Let me explain. Though I firmly believe what the early church and the reformers taught concerning the nature of the Scriptures, and though I would emphasize that what they have to say concerning the Scriptures is crucially important, yet again, truth is finally related to something behind the Scriptures. The Scriptures are important, not because they are printed in a certain way nor bound in a certain kind of leather, nor because they have helped many people. This is not the basic reason for the Scriptures' being overwhelmingly important. The Bible, the historic Creeds and orthodoxy are important because God is there, and, finally, that is the only reason they have their importance.

The force of this was brought home to me several years ago when a young Swiss-German architect was reporting at one of our Farel House seminars in Switzerland on Max Planck's last essays. He pointed out that Planck, speaking in terms of his discipline, which was physics and not religion, said that modern man has had to move the screen back several times in our generation, and the question he posed was: what will be the final screen? Planck was saying that we do not know what the final screen will be in the material structure of the universe. This idea of a final screen started to bore away in my mind as a Christian, and as one speaking into the twentieth-century world.

What is the final screen of truth?

The answer can only be the existence of God and who he is. Therefore, Christian truth is that which is in relationship to what exists and ultimately to the God who exists. And true spirituality consists of being in the correct relationship to the God who is there, first in the once-for-all act of justification, second by being in that correct relationship as a continuing moment-by-moment reality. This is the biblical emphasis on true spirituality. It is a continuing moment-by-moment proper relationship with the God who exists.

The God Behind Truth

I have chosen to use this expression "God is there" as being equivalent to "God exists," not because I am unaware of the theological discussions today, nor because I have met anyone who, holding to the truth of the Bible, believes in a three-story universe, but in order to meet the problem of the modern theology, which denies that God is there in the historical biblical sense. We must have the courage to say that God is there, or to use different terminology, that the final environment of what is there is God himself, the One who has created everything else.

Let us notice carefully that in saying God is there, we are saying God exists, and not just talking about the *word* god or the *idea* god. We are speaking of the proper relationship to the living God who exists. In order to understand the problems of our generation, we should be very alive to this distinction.

Semantics (linguistic analysis) for a certain period made up the heart of modern philosophical study in the Anglo-Saxon world. Though the Christian cannot accept this study as a philosophy, there is no reason why he should not be glad for the concept that words need to be defined before they can be used in communication. As Christians we must understand that there is no word so meaningless as the word *god* until it is defined. No word has been used to teach absolutely opposite concepts as much as the word *god*. Consequently, let us not be confused. There is much "spirituality" about us today that relates itself to the *word* god or to the *idea* god; but this is not what we are talking about. Biblical truth and spirituality is not a relationship to the *word* god, or to the *idea* god. It is a relationship to the One who is there. This is an entirely different concept.

Following on from the discussion as to who or what God is, springs the second fundamental question of today, "Who or what am I?" In order to make it possible to have a meaningful relationship between God and man, an answer to both questions must be given.

The answer we give here profoundly affects our idea of the form of the relationship between God and man. Whether we regard this relationship as mechanical, deterministic or—infinitely more wonderful—personal will turn upon our answers to the questions "Who is the God who is there?" and "Who am I?"

Many sensitive people today are really struggling for their lives, asking the question "What is the purpose of man?" In fact, modern man has not come up with a satisfactory answer to this question in any of his fields of thinking. It does not matter much whether he has approached it along the lines of naked rationalism or the leap into the dark of modern secular and theological mysticism; twentieth-century man has failed to answer this question.

When someone asks me the Christian answer to this question of purpose, the reason for man's existence, I always take them to the first commandment of Christ. In passing, let us note that there is no reason to think that the first commandment—"Thou shalt love the Lord thy God with all thy heart, and with all thy soul, and with all thy mind, and with all thy strength"[1]—is merely a first commandment uttered by Jesus. We know it is not so because he quoted it from the last book of Moses, the book of Deuteronomy. But we can say something more. Surely it is the first commandment because it is the one that expresses the purpose of man and, individually, my purpose.

But it is not enough to quote this on its own. Without the answer given by historic Christianity that God is really there, such an answer can only be another cliché to the honest inquirer, just one more twentieth-century "religious answer"; and we cannot blame him if he stops listening. When I hear this first commandment to love the God who is there with everything that I am, it carries with it a total concept of life and of truth. A man can love only a God who exists and who is personal and about whom he has knowledge. So the fact that this God has communicated is also of supreme importance. But this commandment carries something more; it tells me something very fundamental and exciting about *myself.*

There is indeed something to be excited about if we know the dilemmas of our generation. If you could see the sober, sensitive men and women who come to our chalet asking the question "who, or what, am I?" with real longings, you would realize there is something electrifying to know about "myself."

As far as the modern mentality is concerned, it is shattering to be told that there is nothing intrinsically nonsensical in calling upon me to love the God who is there, and that God is of such a nature and that I am of such a nature as to make this a valid proposition. Those who understand what is involved will not dismiss this as "something I have heard since I was little." To think through the implications is totally exciting. The God who is there is of such a nature that he can be loved, and I am of such a nature that I can love; and thus this first commandment, or basic purpose of man, is the very opposite of a nonsense statement. I know what man is, and I know who I am.

Section Six

Personal &
Corporate Living
into the Twentieth-
Century Climate

1
Demonstrating the Character of God

Salvation Does Not End with the Individual

We have examined the tension which a non-Christian is bound to feel—the tension between the real world and the logical conclusion of a man's non-Christian presuppositions. If we are honest, Christians too have a question to face. As people watch us, individually and corporately, and hear our presuppositions, what do they see with regard to our consistence to our presuppositions?

| The man, now the Christian, and his presuppositions | ⟶ | The logical conclusion of our Christian presuppositions |

In this concluding section I want to pursue the question of a reality which is visible to a watching world.

As Christians we must consider what the logical conclusions of *our* presuppositions are. Here we are speaking of apologetics, not abstractly, not scholastically, not as a subject taught in a Christian school but as practiced in the battles of our generation. Christian apologetics must be able to show intellectually that Christianity speaks of *true truth;* but it must also *exhibit* that it is not just a theory. This is needed for the defense of the flock of Christ, and also in the positive sense of reaching out to those who are honestly asking questions. What is observable, both individually and corporately, is also included in Christian apologetics. Christians should always have comprehended and considered this; but it is overwhelmingly important in view of the thought-forms of our generation to show that Christianity is not just a better dialectic.

As orthodox evangelicals we have often made the mistake of stopping with individual salvation. Historically the word *Christian* has meant two things. First, the word *Christian* defines a person who has accepted Christ as Savior. This is decidedly an individual thing. But there is a second consideration as well. It concerns that which flows from individual salvation. While it is true that there is an individual salvation, and this is the beginning of the Christian life, yet nevertheless individual salvation should show itself also in *corporate* relationships. This is the Bible's clear teaching concerning the church and what we find, in some measure, as we consider the church at its strongest through the ages.

When man fell, various divisions took place. The first and basic division is between man who has revolted and God. All other divisions flow from that. We are separated from God by our guilt—true moral guilt. Hence we need to be justified upon the basis of the finished substitutionary work of the Lord Jesus Christ. Yet it is quite plain from the Scriptures and from general observation that the separations did not stop with the separation of man from God. For, second, man was separated from himself. This gives rise to the psychological problems of life. Third, man was separated from other men, leading to the sociological problems of life. Fourth, man was separated from nature.

According to the teaching of the Scriptures, the finished work of the Lord Jesus Christ is meant eventually to bring healing to each of these divisions: healing which will be perfect in every aspect when Christ comes again in history in the future.

In justification, there is a relationship which is already perfect. When the individual accepts Christ as his Savior, on the basis of the finished work of Christ, God as Judge declares that his guilt is gone immediately and forever. With regard to the other separations, it is plain from the scriptural teaching and from the struggles of God's people throughout the best years of the church that in this present life the blood of Christ is meant to bring *substantial* healing now. Individual salvation comes with justification, and guilt is gone at once. Then comes a future day when my body will be raised from the dead, and the other separations will be healed just as completely. Now, in the present life, when men can observe us, there is to be a *substantial* healing of these other divisions. *Substantial* is the right word to use because it carries with it two ideas. First, it means that it is not yet perfect. Second, it means that there is reality.

The Visible Quality

The world has a right to look upon us and make a judgment. We are told by Jesus that as we love one another the world will judge, not only whether we are his disciples, but whether the Father sent the Son.[1] The final apologetic, along with the rational, logical defense and presentation, is *what the world sees* in the individual Christian and in our corporate relationships together. The command that we should love one another surely means something much richer than merely organizational relationship. Not that we should minimize proper organizational relationship, but one may look at those bound together in an organized group called a church and see nothing of a substantial healing of the division between people in the present life.

On the other hand, while there is "the invisible church" (that is, everyone who is a Christian living anywhere in the world), yet the church is not to be hidden away, in an unseen area, as though it does not matter what men see. What we are called to do, upon the basis of the finished work of Christ in the power of the Spirit through faith, is to exhibit a substantial healing, individual and then corporate, so that people may observe it. This too is a portion of the apologetic: a presentation which gives at least some demonstration that these things are not theoretical but real; not perfect, yet substantial. If we only speak of and exhibit the individual effects of the gospel, the world, psychologically conditioned as it is today, will explain them away. What the world cannot explain away will be a substantial, corporate exhibition of the logical conclusions of the Christian presuppositions. It is not true that the New Testament presents an individualistic concept of salvation. Individual, yes—we must come one at a time, but it is not to be individualistic. First there must be the individual reality, and then the corporate. Neither will be perfect in this life, but they must be real. I have discovered that hard twentieth-century people do not expect Christians to be perfect. They do not throw it in our teeth when, individually or corporately, they find less than perfection in us. They do not expect perfection, but they do expect reality; and they have a right to expect reality, upon the authority of Jesus Christ.

There must be communion and community among the people of God—not a false community that is set up as though human community were an end in itself; but in the local church, in a mission, in a school, wherever it might be, true fellowship must be evident as the outcome of original, individual salvation. This is the real church of the Lord Jesus Christ—not merely organization but a group of people, individually the people of God, drawn together by the Holy Spirit for a particular task either in a local situation or over a wider area. The church of the Lord Jesus should be a group of those who are redeemed and bound together on the basis of true doctrine. But subsequently they should show together a substantial "sociological healing" of the breaches between men which have come about because of the results of man's sin.

The Christian sociological position is that the sociological problems which exist, regardless of what they may be, are a result of the separation that has come between men because of sin. Now the world should be able to see in the church external marks which exhibit that there is a substantial sociological healing possible in the present generation. We can never expect the testimony of a previous generation to be sufficient for our own time. We can point to the wonders of past achievements, but men have a right to say, "This is our moment, this is our history, what about today?" It is not enough for the church to be engaged with the State in healing social ills, though this is important at times. But when the world can turn around and see a group of God's people exhibiting substantial healing in the area of human relationships in their present life, then the world will take notice. Each group of Christians is, as it were, a pilot plant, showing that something can be done in the present situation, if only we begin in the right way.

Corporate living in the early church was very strong at this point. It was not perfect, but it was strong. The testimony has come down to us that one of the things that shook the Roman Empire was that as they looked at these Christians—a cross section of the wide sociological spectrum in the Roman Empire, from slaves to their masters, and including some of Caesar's household—non-Christians were forced to say, "Behold, how they love each other." And this was not in a vacuum, but loving each other in the circle of truth.

Realism in Exhibition

We must look to the Son of God, moment by moment, for these things; such things cannot be done in our own strength. We must allow him to bear his fruit through us. We can proclaim "orthodoxy" in the flesh, and we can compromise in the flesh. But our calling is a different calling: it is to exhibit God and his character, by his grace, in this generation. We need to show him forth as personal, as holy and as love. It is possible in the flesh to be both orthodox and dead—or loving and compromising. What is not possible in the flesh is simultaneously to exhibit both the justice of God and the love of God—this can only be done through the work of the Holy Spirit. And yet anything less is not a picture of God, but only a caricature of the God who exists.

Demonstrating God's character must be existential. The existentialists are right at this place, though they are wrong when they say that history is not going anywhere. As far as living is concerned, we are on the knife-edge of time. What will matter is our relationship to the Lord Jesus, individually and then corporately, at this existential moment. What counts, as men look upon us individually and corporately, is whether we are exhibiting God and his character *now*. The Christian position is not static but is living.

Christ says, "Be ye therefore perfect, even as your Father which is in heaven is perfect."[2] How could a perfect God say, "Just sin a little bit"? This would be impossible. The standard is God's own perfection. And yet the Word of God does not leave us with a romantic notion that we must either have total perfection in this life or, if not, that we must smash everything and have nothing. I am firmly convinced that many wonderful things have been destroyed because people have had a preconceived and romantic notion in their minds as to what the perfect thing should be, would settle for nothing else, and thus have smashed what could have been.

How glad we should be for the apostle John when he says, "My little children, these things write I unto you, that ye sin not. And if any man sin, *we* have an advocate with the Father."[3] There is a tremendous and wonderful implication in that word "*we.*" John, the beloved apostle, places himself among us. On the one hand, we must stand against all standards lower than perfection. The standards are not arbitrary, but are those which the holy God who exists has given us in the Bible, and we are to take them with total seriousness. Anything less than the totality of these standards will not do. Sin is not to be minimized either in the individual or the corporate life. Antinomianism in theory or practice is always wrong and destructive.

Yet, on the other hand, we must stand against all the romantic concepts of perfection in this life. The Bible does not promise us perfection in this life, except in the area of justification. It does not promise us in this life perfection morally, physically, psychologically or sociologically. There are to be moral victories and growth, but that is different from perfection. John could say "we." Paul could indicate his own lack of perfection.[4] There can be physical healing, but that does not mean that the one healed is then a perfect physical specimen. The day Lazarus was raised from the dead he may have had a headache, and certainly one day he died again. People can be wonderfully helped psychologically, but that does not mean that they will then be totally integrated personalities. The Christian position is understanding that on this side of the resurrection the call *is* to perfection, and yet at the same time not to smash and destroy what we cannot bring again to life—just simply because it is less than the perfections that we romantically build in our thinking. For example, how many women have I found—and how many men—who have stomped on a perfectly good marriage until it was dead, just because they had a romantic concept of what marriage should or could be, either physically or emotionally.

Personality Is Central

We have been speaking about those things which are vitally important with regard to the logical conclusions of the Christian presuppositions. So far we have spoken about two, the *corporate* and the *substantial*. Now we will add the third, the *personal*.

The Christian system is consistent as no other system that has ever been. It is beautiful beyond words, because it has that quality that no other system completely has—you begin at the beginning, and you can go to the end. It is as simple as that. *And every part and portion of the system can be related back to the beginning.* Whatever you discuss, to understand it properly, you just go back to the beginning and the whole thing is in its place. The beginning is simply that God exists and that he is the personal-infinite God. Our generation longs for the reality of personality, but it cannot find it. But Christianity says personality is valid because personality has not just appeared in the universe but rather is rooted in the personal God who has always been.

All too often, when we are talking to the lost world, we do not begin at the beginning and therefore the world stops listening. Without this emphasis on personality we cannot expect people really to listen, because without this the concept of salvation is suspended in a vacuum.

If we understand this, we understand the meaning of life. The meaning of life does not end with justification, but is seen in the reality that when we accept Christ as our Savior in the true biblical sense, our personal relationship with the personal God is restored. Every place we turn in Christianity we find that we are brought face to face with the wonder of personality—the very opposite of the dilemma and the sorrow of modern man who finds no meaning in personality. Consider the words of Paul, "The grace of the Lord Jesus Christ, and the love of God, and the communion of the Holy Ghost be with you all."[5] It is the personal to which we are brought. First of all there is the personal relationship with God himself—this is the most wonderful, and is not just in heaven but is substantially real in practice now. When we understand our calling, it is not only true but beautiful—and it should be exciting. It is hard to understand how an orthodox, evangelical, Bible-believing Christian can fail to be excited. The answers in the realm of the intellect should make us overwhelmingly excited. But more than this, we are returned to a personal relationship with the God who is there. If we are unexcited Christians, we should go back and see what is wrong. We are surrounded by a generation that can find "no one home" in the universe. If anything marks our generation, it is this. In contrast to this, as a Christian I know who I am; and I know the personal God who is there. I speak, and he hears. I am not surrounded by mere mass, nor only energy particles, but he is there. And if I have accepted Christ as my Savior, then though it will not be perfect in this life, yet moment by moment, on the basis of the finished work of Christ, this person-to-person relationship with the God who is there can have reality to me.

2
The Legal, but Not Only the Legal

___

*T*oday most non-Christians exclude any real notion of law. They do this because they have no *absolute* anywhere in the universe, and without an absolute one cannot really have any morals as morals. For them everything is relative; they have no real *circle* of law. For them there is no circle inside which there is right, in contrast to that which is outside the circle and therefore wrong. To the Christian this is not so. God does exist, and he has a character; there are things which are outside the commandments he has given us as the expression of his character. For example, there is therefore a proper legal circle in regard to the visible church. The visible church should be a true church. It will not be a perfect church, but it should be a true one. And marriage is the proper circle for sexual relationships. The new morality, following the new theology and lacking the Christian epistemology, the Christian Scripture, and the Christian God, can find no real legal circle and so finds no way to set boundaries.

The fault of orthodoxy is that though it has a legal circle, it tends too often to act as though merely to be within the legal circle is enough. We should be thankful for the legal circle—a real absolute, something we can know and within which we can function—because it means that we do not have to act on the assumption that we can, or must, weigh all the results of our acts out to infinity, when, being finite, we cannot see the results of our acts more than one or two steps ahead. Having to act as a finite god is painful. But what a tragedy to think that because we are in the proper legal circle, everything is finished and done—as though marriage, the church and other human relationships are static and that only the legal circle is important.

Even in justification, many Christians who are perfectly orthodox in doctrine look back upon their justification as though it were the end of all, at least until death comes. It is not. Birth is essential to life, but the parent is not glad only for the birth of his child. He is thankful for the living child that grows up. Whoever saw a couple get engaged simply because they wanted to enjoy the marriage ceremony? What they want to do is to live together. So it is with becoming a Christian. In one way you can say that the new birth is everything; in another way you can say that really it is very little. It is everything because it is indispensable to begin with, but it is little in comparison with the living existential relationship. The legal circle of justification does not end statically; it opens to me a living person-to-person communication with the God who exists.

In marriage, in the church and in other human relationships the same thing applies—the proper legal relationship must be there, but if it is static it becomes a dusty monument. It is no longer beautiful. It becomes a flower that dies under a glass. It can only be beautiful if inside the proper legal circle we have a personal relationship which speaks of the personal God who is there. This is our calling, not only to exhibit something substantially real to a watching world but to enjoy it ourselves. I am called to love God with all my heart and soul and mind, and I am called to love my neighbor as myself: each person involved in the proper circle and in the proper relationship.

If we say that personality is not an intrusion in the universe but central, the world has a right to see the Christians, both individually and corporately, living on a personal level. Men must see that we take personality seriously enough, by the grace of God, to act upon it.

There must be an observable indication of this in the midst of the daily life in this present abnormal world, or we have denied the central Christian presupposition.

Human People in Our Culture

When we use the phrase "it is only human," we are usually referring to something sinful. In this sense, the Christian should feel a calling *not* to be "human"; but in a more profound sense, the Christian is called to exhibit the characteristics of true humanity, because being a man is not intrinsically being sinful man, but being that which goes back before the Fall, to man made in the image of God.

Therefore, Christians in their relationships should be the most *human* people you will ever see. This speaks for God in an age of inhumanity and impersonality and facelessness. When people look at us their reaction should be "These are human people": human because we know that we differ from the animal, the plant and the machine, and that personality is native to what has always been. This is not something only to put forward intellectually—when people observe us their reaction should be "These *are* human people!"

If they cannot look upon us and say, "These are real people," nothing else is enough. Far too often young people become Christians and then search among the church's ranks for real people, and have a hard task finding them. All too often evangelicals are paper people.

If we do not preach these things, talk about them to each other, and teach them carefully from the pulpit and in the Christian classroom, we cannot expect Christians so to act. This has always been important, but it is especially so today because we are surrounded by a world in which personality is increasingly eroded. If we who have become God's children do not show him to be personal in our lives, then in practice we are denying his existence. People should see a beauty among Christians in their practice of the centrality of personal relationships— in the whole spectrum of life and in the whole culture. This is equivalent today, when many think both man and God are dead, to the songs of wonder and exultation in the Old Testament, sung because God is a living God and not a lifeless idol.

On the final day of a series of lectures I was giving at a Christian college some years ago, the president of the Student Council handed me the following letter written on Student Council stationery:

Dear Dr. Schaeffer,

You have helped me a great deal this week to spot some of the reasons for my rebellion against both the evangelical form of orthodoxy, and to some degree against God. For this I can't thank you enough, nor can I thank God enough for helping me to see myself a little more clearly. The difficulty, of course, comes in the implementation of my conclusions into my own being, though I trust this will occur.

I am also concerned about the effect that your messages may have on the rest of the campus and on evangelicalism as a whole. You have asserted that Christianity is both a system, orthodoxy, and a personal association with Christ. As such there are some absolutes which we as Christians can depend on and demand of others if they are to be considered truly Christian. With this I agree, although I may not hold to all the absolutes which you have indicated are necessary for the Christian "system." But the matter which is of concern to me is that there are many here at (———) and in evangelicalism who, because they believe they have true truth, impose their own societal and evangelical, subcultural absolutes on those of us who have had "the roof blown off." The result is that students are often forced into either accepting evangelicalism, with all of its absolutes, be they Victorian or early twentieth-century, or out into total despair. Believe me, sir, when I say there are many at (———) in this position. In fact, this is what has finally driven many into neo-orthodoxy and skepticism.

This brings me to my final point which is simply this: Now that you have succeeded in "blowing the roof off" for some students, and have instructed evangelicalism to go and do likewise, would you please tell us how evangelicalism can eliminate some of these extraneous absolutes which make orthodoxy (as we know it) almost impossible to swallow. How can evangelicals really become the salt of the earth when many of their absolutes forbid them to even come into contact with the earth? How does the evangelical house clean

out enough dust to make it the orthodox house, and then perhaps
we will be relevant to the twentieth-century man?

Very Sincerely,

(———)

Student Council President

I do not think that I would agree with this student in all the details
involved, but I do agree that there is much dust to clear out. Our task
is to deal with the dust, but not to burn down the house in order to
remove it.

Appendix A
The Question of Apologetics

Since *The God Who Is There* was originally published, questions have been asked about my views concerning what is often called "apologetics." I will try to clarify this under three headings: *Apologetics, Rationalism,* and *Evangelism and Lifestyle.*

Apologetics

The answer as to whether I am an apologete depends on how the concept of apologete, or apologetics, is defined.

First, I am not an apologete if that means building a safe house to live in, so that we Christians can sit inside with safety and quiescence. Christians should be out in the midst of the world as both witnesses and salt, not sitting in a fortress surrounded by a moat.

Second, I would quote what has been a part of the text of *The God Who Is There* on page 148 from its original edition onward:

As we turn to consider in more detail how we may speak to men of the twentieth century, we must emphasize first of all that we cannot apply mechanical rules. We, of all people, should realize this, for as Christians we believe that personality really does exist and is important. We can lay down some general principles, but there can be no automatic application. If we are truly personal, as created by God, then each individual will differ from everyone else. Therefore each man must be dealt with as an individual, not as a case or statistic or machine. If we would work with these people, we cannot mechanically apply the things of which we have been speaking in this book. We must look to the Lord in prayer, and to the work of the Holy Spirit, for effective use of these things.

In the light of this I have been mystified at times about what has been said concerning "Schaeffer's apologetics."

I do not believe there is any one apologetic which meets the needs of all people. And as I said in the text of *The God Who Is There,* I did not (and do not) mean that what I wrote in that book should ever be applied mechanically, as a set formula. There is no set formula that meets everyone's need, and if only applied as a mechanical formula, I doubt if it really meets anyone's need—short of an act of God's mercy.

Human nature being what it is, I am sure some people have read *The God Who Is There* or have come to L'Abri and have gone away thinking that what they have learned can be applied mechanically as a formula. I, and we at L'Abri, have tried to do everything we can to dispel this. The quotation I gave from *The God Who Is There* above says this clearly.

When we have the opportunity to talk to the non-Christian, what (if not the formula mentality) should be the dominant consideration? I think this should be love. I think these things turn on love and compassion to people, not as objects to evangelize but as people who deserve all the love and consideration we can give them, because they are our kind and made in the image of God. They are valuable, so we should meet them in love and compassion. Thus, we meet the person where he or she is.

Consequently, if I were with Paul and Silas in the Philippian jail, and the Philippian jailer said to me, "Sir, what must I do to be saved?" for me to start talking about epistemology would be horrible. I would say what Paul said: "Believe on the Lord Jesus Christ, and you shall be saved," because the jailer was, on the basis of previous knowledge and events, ready for that answer.[1]

Now on the other hand, if we are dealing with someone who has honest problems and who really believes that truth is truth—things are true and things are false (and that previously was the generally accepted concept almost everywhere)—it would then be a different need. In that situation, if he or she had questions on the historicity of Christ's resurrection and so on, we would deal with those questions—because he or she already accepts that truth is truth.

What I try to do in *The God Who Is There* is to show that when we get to those holding the concept that there is no such thing as objective (or universal) truth, we can still keep talking. We can move further back and keep talking in the way they need. I do not believe that there is any one system of apologetics that meets the need of all people, any more than I think there is any one form of evangelism that meets the need of all people. It is to be shaped on the basis of love for the person as a person.

If we are to deal with people where they are (whether they can express their position in a sophisticated way or not), we have got to have enough genuine love for them and concern, as a human being, that we would take seriously what they are preoccupied with. We tend to give a person a prepackaged answer instead of having the compassion of Christ, which is to take the person where they are and actually step into their world in order to talk in a meaningful way to them. And if that world is that of the Philippian jailer, good; if it is that of the one who believes truth is truth, good; but if it is the person who is lost in relativity, we can give them the Christian answers there as well.

If people do not have "modern" intellectual questions, there is no need of dealing with such questions; but we must acknowledge that in our generation almost everybody has them. I walked out of a restaurant one morning a few weeks ago, and there was a girl sitting with a cup of coffee reading Skinner's book *Beyond Freedom and Dignity*. She represents millions. We have millions and millions facing these questions, and in fact I think today the majority of the community have such questions. And they do not have to be university graduates. I have worked with shipyard workers, mill workers, all kinds of people (as well as, when I was younger, personally working on farms, a huckster wagon, in factories, and so on), and I am convinced that these people often have the same questions as the intellectual; the only thing is that they do not articulate them, or if they do articulate them it is not in the same terminology. I know these people, and I am convinced that the things we are talking about can be talked about to almost anyone—all one has to do is to shift gears in language. Incidentally, that too is love.

The middle-class family wonders why things have changed—they realize the problem of relativism, though they perhaps would not use that term. They are brought up against the relativism when their daughter goes off to sleep with someone, and it is clear that she does not see this as either wrong nor a surprising thing to do. They also see the law changing and do not know why, but are troubled. They too are asking the same questions. They too are either below "the line of despair" or comprehending its existence in some at least vague way. Love means dealing with them at the place where they are.

For the "modern person" we can keep talking in a way which helps because in contrast to the concept that everything is relative, we know that there are good, adequate and sufficient reasons to know that the Christian answers are truth. I do not believe that there is a leap of faith needed; there are good and sufficient reasons to know why Christianity is true—and more than that, that is the Bible's insistence. The Bible's emphasis is that there are good and sufficient reasons to *know* that Christianity is true, so much so that we are disobedient and guilty if we do not believe it.

The Christian system (what is taught in the whole Bible) is a unity of thought. Christianity is not just a lot of bits and pieces—there is a beginning and an end, a whole system of truth, and this system is the only system that will stand up to all the questions that are presented to us as we face the reality of existence. Some of the other systems answer some of the questions but leave others unanswered. I believe it is only Christianity that gives the answers to all the crucial questions.

What are those questions? The questions are those which are presented to us as we face the reality of existence. God shuts us up to reality. We cannot escape the reality of what is, no matter what we say we believe or think.

This reality of which I speak falls into two parts: the fact that the universe truly exists and it has a form, and then what I would call the "mannishness" of man—which is my own term for meaning that man is unique. People have certain qualities that must be explained.

God has shut up all people to these things, and I always like to go back to the statement of Jean-Paul Sartre, though he had no answer for his own statement, and that is that the basic philosophic question is that something is there. Things do exist, and this demands an explanation for their existence. I would then go beyond Sartre's statement to one by Einstein. Einstein said that the most amazing thing about the universe is that we can know something truly about it. In other words, it has a form that is comprehensible, even though we cannot exhaust it. And then I would say beyond that—no matter what people say they are, they are what they are; that is, man is unique as made in the image of God. Any system of thought, to be taken seriously, has to at least try to explain these two great phenomena of the universe and man. In other words, we are talking about objective truth related to reality and not just something within our own heads.

Now I would like to add a corollary to this: In *Whatever Happened to the Human Race?* and especially the extensive notes of the fifth chapter, there is a third thing, and that is the way the Bible measures up to history. Once we say that, this is very exciting. It is very exciting because other religions are not founded in history, they are "out there" somewhere, or you can think of them as inside of your own head—whichever way you are looking at it. On the other hand, the Bible claims to be rooted in history. Whether we are considering the history of the Old Testament, whether we are considering the history of Christ, including the resurrection, or Paul's journeys, it is insisted on as real history. So now we have three interwoven parts. Usually I have dealt with the first two because I think they are the two which touch more the twentieth-century person, but the third is also there. We have to face the reality of the universe and its having an existence and having a form. We have to face the reality in the uniqueness of man. We are able to discuss the fact that the Bible is rooted in history.

I would repeat, God shuts everyone up to the fact of reality, and everyone has to deal with the reality that is.

When we turn to the Bible, the Bible says that on the basis of God's created world and on the basis of who we are, there are good and sufficient reasons to know the biblical answers are true. People come to the knowledge that this is adequate on different levels, depending on their intelligence, their education, their personality, the way their mind works; but at some point they come to the place where indeed they have what to them should be good and sufficient and adequate answers.

So what you have is the flow of the totality of reality—instead of being focused on religious things only, it is religious things as a part of reality. And instead of this concept being contrary to the Bible, it is the way the Bible is written. It is not "just a religious book"; the Bible is rooted in space-time history and speaks of the totality of reality.

The glory of the Bible is that it is enough for every age and it is enough for every person. When you consider the early chapters of Genesis on through Deuteronomy, given about 1500 B.C. to Moses, it gave truth to those people in that day. Now we come to our age, and we know a lot that those people did not know about the cosmos, all kinds of things, and those same chapters (and the rest of the Bible) are enough to give truth to us. If Christ does not come back for another 500 years, the people then will know more than we do now, and the Bible will give truth to them. So whether it is the individual, no matter what his level of education, sophistication, etc., or whether it is the age we live in with the knowledge we have, the Bible is enough to give the answer to the questions raised by reality.

When people refuse God's answer, they are living against the revelation of the universe and against the revelation of themselves. They are denying the revelation of God in *who* they themselves are. I am not saying that non-Christians do not live in the light of real existence. I am saying that they do not have any answer for living in it. I am not saying that they do not have moral motions, but they have no basis for them. I am not saying that the person with a non-Christian system (even a radical system like Buddhism or Hinduism or the modern Western thinking of chance) does not know that the object exists—the problem is that they have no system to explain the subject-object correlation. As a matter of fact, this is their damnation, this is their tension, that they have to live in the light of their existence, the light of reality—the total reality in all these areas—and they do live there, and yet they have no sufficient explanation for any of these areas. So the wiser they are, the more honest they are, the more they feel that tension, and that is their present damnation.

There is nowhere that people can go that they can escape the things of grace that God has given them to shut them in, in the reality that exists. And if we love people enough and we have compassion enough, we can usually find ways to talk to them, no matter how deep in the well they are. That is what I am saying. It is not that we use a universal formula to reach people, either in evangelism or in apologetics.

When we say a person is lost we usually think of evangelically lost, that he or she is a sinner and needs to accept Christ as Savior. But what we must realize is that these people do not know that they are lost evangelically. How could they? They do not believe there is right and wrong, they do not believe there is a God, they do not believe there is an absolute, there is no reason for them to think of themselves as a sinner. Few believe in guilt anymore. There is only "sickness" or "guilt-feelings" or "sociological nonconformity." There is no such thing as true guilt. How much meaning does our talking about accepting Christ as Savior have for such a person? But our whole generation has a second sense of being lost which is valid, and that is they are without meaning in the world, without purpose, without morals, without a basis for law—no final principles, no final answers for anything. They know they are lost in this way. When we turn to the Bible, the Bible makes plain that indeed they are lost in both senses—they are lost evangelically; but without God they are lost in the modern sense as well.

This lostness is answered by the existence of a Creator. So Christianity does not begin with "accept Christ as Savior." Christianity begins with "In the beginning God created the heavens [the total of the cosmos] and the earth." That is the answer to the twentieth century and its lostness. At this point we are then ready to explain the second lostness (the original cause of all lostness) and the answer in the death of Christ.

In summary: God in his grace has shut us up by the totality of reality to the biblical answers—i.e., there are good, adequate and sufficient reasons to know that the Christian answers are truth—so much so that if we do not bow to those answers, the Bible says we are disobedient and guilty.

Those who object to the position that there are good, adequate and sufficient reasons to *know with our reason* that Christianity is true are left with a *probability position* at some point. At some point and in some terminology they are left with a leap of faith. This does not say that they are not Christians, but it means that they are offering *one more probability* to twentieth-century relativistic people to whom everything is only probability. They are offering one more leap of faith without reason (or with the severe diminishing of reason) to a generation that has heard a thousand leaps of faith proposed in regard to the crucial things of human life. I would repeat that what is left is that Christianity is a probability.

Of course, faith is needed to become a Christian, but there are two concepts concerning faith. The two ideas of faith run like this: One idea of faith would be a blind leap in the dark. A blind leap in which you believe something with no reason (or no adequate reason), you just believe it. This is what I mean by a blind leap of faith. The other idea of faith, which has no relationship with this, none whatsoever, is that you are asked to believe something and bow before that something on the basis of good and adequate reasons. There is no relationship between those two concepts of faith.

The biblical concept of faith is very much the second and not the first. You are not asked to believe in a blind leap of faith. The Bible teaches that there are good and sufficient reasons to know that these things are true. If you examine the ministry of Paul and also of Christ, you find they endlessly answered questions. There was no concept here of "Keep quiet, just believe"; it just does not exist. Paul answered the questions of the Jews, he answered the questions of the non-Jews, he was always answering questions; and the book of Romans certainly answered the questions of those without the Bible as well as of those with it.

There are good and sufficient reasons to know that these things are true. We have already dealt with the fact of reality and everybody having to deal with reality: (1) the existence of the universe and its form; (2) the distinctiveness of man; and (3) you can relate these to a third thing, and that is the examination of the historicity of Scripture.

But now we can ask another question. If it is so that there are good and sufficient reasons to know that Christianity is true, why doesn't everybody accept the sufficient answers?

We must realize that Christianity is the easiest religion in the world, because it is the only religion in which God the Father and Christ and the

Holy Spirit do everything. God is the Creator; we have nothing to do with our existence or the existence of other things. We can shape other things, but we cannot change the fact of existence. We do nothing for our salvation because Christ did it all. We do not have to do anything. In every other religion we have to do something—everything from burning a joss stick to sacrificing our firstborn child to dropping a coin in the collection plate—the whole spectrum. But with Christianity we do not do anything; God has done it all. He has created us and he has sent his Son; his Son died and because the Son is infinite, therefore he bears our total guilt. We do not need to bear our guilt, nor do we even have to merit the merit of Christ. He does it all. So in one way it is the easiest religion in the world.

But now we can turn that over because it is the hardest religion in the world for the same reason. The heart of the rebellion of Satan and man was the desire to be autonomous; and accepting the Christian faith robs us not of our existence, not of our worth (it gives us our worth), but it robs us completely of being autonomous. We did not make ourselves, we are not a product of chance, we are none of these things; we stand there before a Creator plus nothing, we stand before the Savior plus nothing—it is a complete denial of being autonomous. Whether it is conscious or unconscious (and in the most brilliant people it is occasionally conscious), when they see the sufficiency of the answers on their own level, they suddenly are up against their innermost humanness—not humanness as they were created to be human but human in the bad sense since the Fall. That is the reason that people do not accept the sufficient answers and why they are counted by God as disobedient and guilty when they do not bow.

People are living against the revelation of themselves. They are denying the revelation of God that they themselves and all reality are. They are denying it, and yet they have to live with it. When the person comes to see that there are good and sufficient reasons, then he or she is faced with a problem; either they bow before those good and sufficient reasons, *and bow to the Person behind the reasons*, or they refuse to bow.

It is not that the answers are not good, adequate and sufficient. Unless one gives up one's autonomy, one *cannot* accept the answers.

Rationalism

At times some have said my way of discussing "apologetics" is a form of rationalism.

First, a definition of words is helpful: A *rationalist* is someone who thinks man can begin with himself and his reason plus what he observes, without information from any other source, and come to final answers in regard to truth, ethics and reality. In contrast to the words *rationalist* and *rationalism*, *rationality* concerns the validity of thought, or the possibility to reason.

Some who have said I am a rationalist also speak of my being Aristotelian—that is, that my thinking has been influenced by Aristotle. Those who do this usually (if not always) would hold the position that thought in terms of antithesis was originated by Aristotle. Thought in terms of antithesis means the concept that if a certain thing is true, the opposite is not true; or if a certain thing is right, the opposite is wrong. It would be well here for you to rethink all I have said about antithesis in *The God Who Is There* and also in *Escape from Reason*. In *The God Who Is There*, my note 5 on section 3, chapter 3, in regard to Heidegger, is important concerning this discussion.

Heidegger and others who hold the view that rational thought in terms of antithesis began with Aristotle have no historic basis for this. Rational thought as antithesis is not rooted in Aristotle, it is rooted in reality: first, the reality of the objective existence of God in antithesis to his now existing; second, the reality that God is a personal-infinite God to whom not all things are the same, in antithesis to an impersonal or limited God, or one who does not differentiate in the areas of truth or morals; third, the reality of the objective existence of that which God created in contrast to what he did not create; fourth, that which people do or make or paint or think, etc., in contrast to what does not exist. In morals, antithesis rests upon what conforms to God's character, in contrast to what opposes it.

Further, our minds are so created by God that we think in antithesis, so much so that the only way a person can deny antithesis is on the basis of antithesis. It is not surprising that God made our minds to think in the category of antithesis, for this fits the reality of his existence and the reality of his creation.

When certain people speak of those who hold to rationality (in regard to the Christian answers being adequate and sufficient) as being Aristotelian or rationalistic, they themselves should go back and think through as to whether they are not trapped in irrationality, not only in this discussion but in other areas as well.

As I said above, a rationalist is a person who thinks man and his reason can come to final answers without information from any other source. No one stresses more than I that people have no final answers in regard to truth, morals or epistemology without God's revelation in the Bible. This is true in philosophy, science and theology. Rationalism can take a secular or theological form. In both, the rationalist thinks that on the basis of man's reason, plus what he can see about him, final answers are possible. My books stress that man cannot generate final answers from himself. First, even without the Fall, man was finite and needed the knowledge God gave him (revelation). Second, on this side of the Fall this is even more necessary.

At this point I would suggest you reread my illustration of the torn book in *The God Who Is There*. As Christians, we do have the answers to the questions posed by reality. But we have not thought up these answers, we did not generate the answers, we are not the origin of the answers—we know them from God's revelation. This is the very opposite of rationalism.

On the other hand, the Bible does not say man is a zero. This view would be that since the Fall man cannot do anything, he just sits there and suddenly there is a strike of lightning out of the sky and he is a Christian. But the Bible does not say that. As I have said, the Bible stresses that the individual is guilty before God if he does not bow in the light of the adequacy of the biblical answers to the questions posed by reality. The individual has the responsibility of bowing before the answers which reason indicates to be sufficient *and necessary.*[2]

The work of the Holy Spirit and the responsibility I have as made in the image of God cannot be put into a Cartesian, mathematical formula. But that is different from saying, on one hand, that man can find the final answers by his finite (and fallen) reason alone, or on the other hand, that man as he now is, is a zero. The Bible rejects both of these positions.

And as we speak of the balance of the work of the Holy Spirit and the person's responsibility to be humble enough to give up his or her autonomy to bow to the adequate answers, so also as we give the adequate and sufficient answers (which we did not generate, but which we have from the Bible), we must consciously pray for the Lord's work as these adequate answers are given. Giving the answers does not stand in a dichotomy with our being careful not to minimize the work of the Holy Spirit. When I am talking to an individual or sitting on a platform talking to 5,000 people and answering questions, very often, more often than most people know, I am praying for them. There is no contradiction between such prayer with expectancy that the Lord will answer that prayer, and showing that the Bible gives such good, adequate, sufficient and necessary answers to the questions raised by reality that the hearers are truly disobedient and guilty if they do not bow.

Evangelism and Lifestyle

People often say, "What are you?" and I at times have said, "Well, basically I am an evangelist." But sometimes I do not think people have understood that does not mean that I think of an evangelist in contrast to dealing with philosophic, intellectual or cultural questions with care.

I am not a professional, academic philosopher—that is not my calling, and I am glad I have the calling I have, and I am equally glad some other people have the other calling. But when I say I am an evangelist, it is not that I am thinking that my philosophy, etc. is not valid—I think it is. For example, the answer I give in *He Is There and He Is Not Silent*, I think, is the real answer in regard to epistemology. That is not to say that all my answers are correct. Nor is it to say that the more academically oriented philosopher cannot deal with more of the necessary details. But what I am saying is that all the cultural, intellectual or philosophic material is not to be separated from leading people to Christ. I think my talking about metaphysics, morals and epistemology to certain individuals is a part of my evangelism just as much as when I get to the moment to show them that they are morally guilty and tell them that Christ died for them on the cross. I do not see or feel a dichotomy: *this* is my philosophy and *that* is my evangelism. The whole thing is evangelism to the people who are caught in the second lostness we spoke of—the second lostness being that they do not have any answers to the questions of meaning, purpose and so on.

We always should realize, and I cannot say it often enough, that Christianity is a creation-centered teaching. It is not that suddenly for some strange reason out of nowhere if you accept Christ as Savior you are in. That is a part of a total structure. Christianity is a *system*, and I would say that I have no apology for using the word *system*, though it must not be allowed to be a mere academic system or theoretical or dead intellectualism. In the proper sense of the word, God is systematic in His creation and revelation.

It has got to be the whole man coming to know this is truth, acting upon it, living it out in his life and worshiping God. But it is a system, it begins with the fact that there is a Creator, there is the God, the triune God who has existed forever. He has created all things, so there is nothing autonomous from him.

Thus apologetics, as I see it, should not be separated in any way from evangelism. In fact, I wonder if "apologetics" which does not lead people to Christ as Savior, and then on to their living under the lordship of Christ in the whole of life, really is Christian apologetics. There certainly is a place for an academic study of a subject called "apologetics," as the defense and the credibility of Christianity, but if it does not lead the students to use that material in the way I have spoken about in the previous sentence, one can ask its value.

There certainly is a place for a study of philosophy as a scholarly discipline in great detail. That too can be a Christian's calling. But if the total course does not give answers so that the students are left with more than probability in regard to Christianity, it is much less than a course in philosophy can and should be.

To me there is a unity of all reality, and we can either say that every field of study is a part of evangelism (especially useful to certain people in the world); or we can say that there is no true evangelism that does not touch all of reality and all of life.

There are those who would approve (and praise) the "lifestyle," the emphasis on community, at L'Abri, but who would strenuously differ with what is taught here. Their disapproval usually falls somewhere under what I have dealt with above under the headings of *Apologetics, Rationalism* and *Evangelism and Lifestyle.*

Certainly there is no perfection of community at L'Abri, but we are thankful for what there has been (and is) in it of reality and beauty.

To us what there has been of the reality of community *is living truthfully* upon what the truth is. Without the certainty of that truth, and the content of that truth, the call for community would float in midair and be one more utopia. What there has been of the reality of community rests upon what is taught here.

Our calling is not primarily to an alternate lifestyle. Considering what the Bible teaches, what is crucial is not the word *community,* nor the form the practice of community takes.

Our primary calling is to truth as it is rooted in God, his acts and revelation; and if it is indeed truth, it touches all of reality and all of life, including an adequate basis for, and some practice of, the reality of community.

1981

Appendix B
The Problem of the Middle-Class Church in the Latter Half of the Twentieth Century

It is my hope that this book may be useful in helping orthodox evangelicalism so that it will be a thing of strength and beauty in the second half of the twentieth century.

In order for evangelicalism to be this, three principles must be observed:

1. The full doctrinal position of historic Christianity must be clearly maintained.

2. Every honest question must be given an honest answer. It is unbiblical for anyone to say, "Just believe."

3. There must be an individual and corporate exhibition that God exists in our century, in order to show that historic Christianity is more than just a superior dialectic or a better point of psychological integration.

There are two sections of our society to which, by and large, we have failed to communicate—the intellectuals on the one hand, and the workers on the other. The problem of being largely middle-class in our churches becomes really pressing both because of this, and also when we realize that we are losing children of Christian parents because they no longer accept their middle-class background in either home or local church.

In the two increasingly important areas of ideas and the application of morals, the majority of churches have little to say either to intellectuals or workers or, too often, to the young people from Christian homes.

Working in Switzerland, we have had many Christians' children who are honestly confused, coming from many different countries. They find so often that the answers they have been given simply do not touch the problems which are *their* problems. But this observation is gleaned not only from the many people who come to us in Switzerland but also from traveling over much of the Western world, lecturing in many different places.

It is therefore my considered opinion that if the church today is really concerned to break out of its middle-class format and meet the intellectuals, workers and young people where they are, it must make an honest and courageous attempt to implement all three of the principles above. It is as we who are working together in L'Abri Fellowship have sought by the grace of God, even though totally inadequately, to put them into practice that we have seen many twentieth-century men and women reached by the gospel. It would be our conclusion that all three points are imperative, wherever the church is serious in wanting to speak to these of our generation.

We do not think that the material and outlook in this book is shut up to a few exotic Christian works appealing to an international group of intellectual and creative people. A number of those who have spent time to grasp this material are now using it with the uneducated with very encouraging results. For this we are thankful.

But even more, we are convinced that a comprehending use of this material would be helpful also within the "middle-class" churches and institutions which make up so much of evangelicalism and orthodoxy today. First, it would give a new dimension of wealth in Christ to those churches, missions and institutions. Second, it would be much harder for those round about to write them off as a subculture representing largely only yesterday. Third, they would protect their own next generation. The Christians have been in danger not only of not understanding but of not taking seriously the problems of their children.

I must say that I am deeply troubled not only by what I find among our Western churches, but also by what I come up against among Christian converts from overseas. On many occasions as I have been lecturing to international groups, I have felt torn to bits for those from overseas who have been educated in mission schools and then sent out naked into the twentieth-century world.

The work of the Holy Spirit should never be minimized, but nowhere in the Scriptures do we find the work of the Holy Spirit an excuse for laziness and lack of love on the part of those with Christian responsibility. Nor is the Holy Spirit ever old-fashioned in the bad meaning of that term.

A word of warning here. To grasp and apply the principles we have been seeking to lay down is not just to memorize a static framework or terminology; this could be just one more dead thing. One of the joys in our work is to see how many young people and more mature teachers are carrying this thinking into their own academic disciplines and the arts, and are developing them along the lines of their own fields of interest.

As we seek to meet the problems there are two things which we must strenuously seek to avoid, whether we are engaged in teaching, missionary work or in some aspect of the life of the local church.

First: settling down and accepting the present situation simply because of the inertia caused by those who speak of the problem of the churches' young people and speak much of missions, but who simply do not want to question the familiar because it is painful to do so. The problem is that the evangelical, orthodox churches, institutions and programs are today often under the control of those who are in this category. This control is both organizational and financial. Thus, there is a tendency not to "rock the boat." This responsibility cannot be met by the young people themselves nor by the young ministers and young missionaries alone.

Mature Christians, and Christians in places of responsibility, must summon the courage to distinguish, under the Holy Spirit, between unchangeable biblical truth and the things which have merely become comfortable for us. Often one hears people speak of "the simple gospel only," when in reality they do not really care enough for those outside the churches, or their own children for that matter, to be willing to face what preaching the simple gospel may mean in a changing and complex situation.

Second: the development of an intellectual and cultural snobbishness or elitism. This can easily come about unless we help one another not to fall into it. Such an attitude grieves the Holy Spirit, destroys rather than builds and is as offensively ugly as anything can be.

We will make mistakes, but by God's grace we must strive to avoid either of these two errors or a choice between them.

After considerable thought and the practical experience of trying it out in several countries, I would suggest the following two concepts be borne in mind as we train our young people to take their full part in the Christian work of our time.

First of all, it must be remembered that those who make up the body of the churches and the institutions are also the lambs of God. They need care and help just as much as do the intellectuals, the creative people and the young people who are becoming twentieth-century people. When a pastor accepts the call to go to a particular church, his call is to minister to the whole congregation. Those who care nothing about the new problems are to be fed and shepherded. Therefore, the general preaching and teaching in the middle-class evangelical church should not be of such a nature as to confuse, hurt or undernourish them.

On the other hand, nothing should be preached or taught in the general services and classes which will have to be unlearned when young people and others read and discuss the deeper problems or go away to university. I would suggest that all Sunday school, Bible class and educational material should be prepared with this in mind. We should ask ourselves the question "Is the material of such a nature that it could be extended by eighteen years of honest study without it proving false?"

This will mean more attention to the preparation of sermons, lesson material, Bible study notes and so on. Not everyone will be equally adept at this, but each could be helped if Christian schools, seminaries and theological colleges, Bible schools, missionary training institutes, and publishing houses would set up a program in order to avoid making the old mistakes and omissions and add some to their staff who had been trained to think in a total cultural apologetic. The program could be set up to be operative at a given date, say in three years' time.

Thus, my first suggestion would be: the general teaching and preaching should be of such a nature as to feed and care for those who make up the body of the congregation or institution, yet keeping in mind that nothing is given which must be unlearned as deeper problems are later met.

Second, I would suggest that special times be set aside in the church, institution or mission, so that those who are in, or are coming into, the twentieth-century problems can get what they need. The occasion could be a talk, discussion or seminar. It would be valuable if those claiming no affiliation to the church could be brought into the discussion as well. It does not have to be a big gathering or extensively publicized, but rather the gathering together of those in the church and outside the church who wish to get on. Nor does this getting on have to be purely intellectual, for if one goes deep enough into the intellectual questions, one comes to the deep spiritual problems and realities. And when one goes deep enough spiritually, one touches on the real intellectual problems and realities.

Men and women trained in this way will then have the opportunity, as they go overseas or into unfamiliar territories at home, of understanding what are the twentieth-century problems people face.

So it seems to me that a course in homiletics or apologetics which does not consciously seek to implement these two suggestions today is really a preparation for failure and sorrow.

Christian conferences, etc., could have a place for caring for those considerations on a deeper and extended level. Surely, too, those who have a responsibility for Christian radio programs and television could at least find small corners for those who, in many places, make up the majority of the population.

In this way all could be fed, and, if introduced not too rapidly but rather with much emphasis on spiritual growth and love as well as understanding, in most cases there would not have to be two "churches" under one roof, nor an explosion.

Yet, I would say, some ripples are worthwhile rather than allowing those outside and our own young people who are longing for real answers to choke in the all-too-present dustiness.

Appendix C
The Practice of Truth

With regard to the first of the principles of which we spoke at the beginning of appendix B *(The full doctrinal position of historic Christianity must be clearly maintained)*, it seems to me that the central problem of evangelical orthodoxy in the second half of the twentieth century is the problem of the *practice* of this principle. This is especially so when we take into account the spiritual and intellectual mentality which is dominant in our century. Any consideration of methods and programs must be secondary to a consideration of this central problem.

If a clear and unmistakable emphasis on truth, in the sense of antithesis, is removed, two things occur: first, Christianity in the next generation as true Christianity is weakened; and second, we shall be communicating only with that diminishing portion of the community which still thinks in terms of the older concept of truth. We are not minimizing the work of the Holy Spirit. We should remember, however, that our responsibility is so to communicate that those who hear the gospel will understand it. If we do not communicate clearly on the basis of antithesis, many will respond to their own interpretation of the gospel, in their own relativistic thought-forms, including a concept of psychological guilt-feelings rather than of true moral guilt before the holy, living God. If they do respond in this way, they have not understood the gospel; they are still lost, and we have defaulted in our task of preaching and communicating the gospel to our generation.

The unity of orthodox or evangelical Christianity should be centered around this emphasis on *truth*. It is always important, but doubly so when we are surrounded by so many for whom the concept of truth, in the sense of antithesis, is considered to be totally unthinkable.

In such a setting the problem of communication is serious; it can only be overcome by negative statements that clearly say what we do *not* mean, so that the twentieth-century man understands the positive statements we *do* mean. Moreover, in an age of synthesis, men will not take our protestations of truth seriously unless they see by our actions that we *practice* truth and antithesis in the unity we try to establish, and in our activities. Without this, in an age of relativity, we cannot expect the evangelical, orthodox church to mean much to the surrounding culture or even to the church's own children. What we try to say in our teaching and evangelism will be understood in the twentieth-century thought-form of synthesis. Both a clear comprehension of the importance of truth and a clear practice of it, even when it is costly to do so, is imperative if our witness and our evangelism are to be significant in our own generation and in the flow of history.

It would seem to me that some evangelicals are jettisoning any serious attempt to exhibit truth and antithesis. There has been a tendency to move from a lack of seriousness ecclesiastically concerning truth to the same tendency in matters of wider cooperation. This often finishes up by denying, in practice if not in theory, the importance of doctrinal truth as such.

Many evangelicals who are rightly disturbed by the new theology's view of the Scriptures and universalism and who try to meet it at these points of error in fact never go far enough back in order to establish a clear line of truth and error which will hold weight for the next generation. Inevitably the next generation tends to go further in the direction already established and, if this is already towards synthesis, they will move with it ever closer to the new theology. Therefore, to avoid this, we must be careful to consider what truth and antithesis mean *in practice* in ecclesiastical matters and in evangelism.

Thus it must be said that in spite of (and even because of) one's commitment to evangelism and cooperation among Christians, I can visualize times when the only way to make plain the seriousness of what is involved in regard to a service or an activity where the gospel is going to be preached is *not* to accept an official part if men whose *doctrine* is known to be an enemy are going to be invited to participate officially. In an age of relativity, the *practice* of truth when it is costly is the only way to cause the world to take seriously our protestations concerning truth. Cooperation and unity that do not lead to purity of life and purity of doctrine are just as faulty and incomplete as an orthodoxy which does not lead to a concern for, and a reaching out towards, those who are lost.

There is an opposite danger to be avoided. Some of those who have contended for truth have cut the ground from under this position, not only by a loss of beauty and love but even, in practice, by a loss of truth in speaking about men.

All too often the only antithesis we have exhibited to the world and to our own children has been our *talking* about holiness or our *talking* about love, rather than the *practice* of holiness and love together as truth, in antithesis to what is false in theology, in the church and the surrounding culture.*

*Based on a talk given at the Berlin Congress on the Bible.

Glossary

Absolute. A concept which is not modifiable by factors such as culture, individual psychology or circumstances, but which is perfect and unchangeable. Used as an antithesis of relativism.

Agnostic. A person who does not know, or who thinks it is impossible to know, whether there is a God.

Anthropology. That which deals only with man, his relationship with himself and with other men, such as the studies of psychology, and sociology, and nothing beyond man.

Antinomianism. Holding that, under the gospel dispensation, the moral law is of no use or obligation.

Antiphilosophy. Many of the modern forms of philosophy which have given up any attempt to find a rational unity to the whole of thought and life.

Antithesis. Direct opposition of contrast between two things. (As in "joy" which is the antithesis of "sorrow.")

Apologetics. That branch of theology having to do with the defense and communication of Christianity.

Archetype. The psychologist Jung interpreted dream symbols that have appeared throughout the history of man and called them archetypes.

Atheist. A person who believes that there is no God.

Authenticate oneself. A term used by existentialists whereby man validates the genuineness of his existence by an act of the will or a feeling of dread.

Being. A term denoting the area of existence.

Communication. The transmitting of ideas and information.

Connotation. The implication of meanings to words other than the definition of the word.

Cosmology. Theory of the nature and principles of the universe.

Dada. The name given to a modern art movement originating in Zurich in 1916. The name, chosen at random from a French dictionary, means "rocking horse."

Determinism. The doctrine that human action is not free but results from such causes as psychological and chemical makeup, which render free will an illusion.

Dialectic. The principle of change which takes place by means of triadic movement. A thesis has its opposite, an antithesis. The two opposites are resolved in a synthesis, which in turn becomes a thesis and the process goes on.

Dichotomy. Division into two totally separated parts. In this book, it is used for the total separation of the rational and logical in man from both meaning and faith.

Epistemology. That part of philosophy concerned with the theory of knowledge, its nature, limits and validity.

Existential. Relating to and dealing with moment-by-moment human existence. Empirical reality as opposed to mere theory.

Existentialism. A modern theory of man that holds that human experience is not describable in scientific or rational terms. Existentialism stresses the need to make vital choices by using man's freedom in a contingent and apparently purposeless world.

Final Experience. Term used by Karl Jaspers to denote a crucial experience which is great enough to give hope of meaning.

Humanism. There are two meanings: (1) Any philosophy or system of thought that begins with man alone, in order to try to find a unified meaning to life; (2) that part of humanistic thinking in the above wider sense that stresses the hope of an optimistic future for mankind.

Impressionism. Movement in the visual arts in which the classical tendencies of nineteenth-century French painting culminated and from which modern art has sprung. Its aim was to reproduce, by means of a careful analysis of color, the effect of light upon objects in nature.

Linguistic Analysis. Branch of philosophy which desires to preserve philosophy from confusion of concepts by showing the use of these concepts in their natural language context. It sees the task of philosophy as clarifying what lies on the surface rather than offering explanations.

Logic. The science of correct reasoning. The predictable and inevitable consequence of rational analysis. In classical logic it could be asserted that "A" is "A" and that "A" cannot equal "non-A."

Logical Positivism. Name given to an analytic trend in modern philosophy which holds that all metaphysical theories are strictly meaningless because, in the nature of the case, unverifiable by reference to empirical facts.

"Mannishness" of Man. Those aspects of man, such as significance, love, rationality and the fear of nonbeing, which mark him off from animals and machines and give evidence of his being created in the image of a personal God.

Methodology. Study of the procedures and principles whereby the question of truth and knowledge is approached.

Monolithic. Constituting one undifferentiated whole. In terms of modern culture, giving a unified message.

Mysticism. There are two meanings: (1) a tendency to seek direct communion with ultimate reality of "the divine" by immediate intuition, insight or illumination; (2) a vague speculation without foundation.

Neo-orthodoxy. Name given to the theology of men who have particularly applied the dialectical methodology of Hegel and Kierkegaard's "leap" to the Christian faith.

Nihilism. A denial of all objective grounds for truth. A belief that existence is basically senseless and useless, leading often to destructive tendencies in society or in the individual.

Pantheism. Doctrine that God and nature are identical. The universe is an extension of God's essence rather than a special creation.

Pragmatism. A system of thought which makes the practical consequences of a belief the sole test of truth.

Presupposition. A belief or theory which is accepted before the next step in logic is developed. Such a prior postulate often consciously or unconsciously affects the way a person subsequently reasons.

Propositional Truth. Truth which can be communicated in the form of a statement in which a predicate or object is affirmed or denied regarding a subject.

Rational. Whatever is related to or based upon man's power to reason consistently.

Rationalism. Cf. Humanism, first meaning.

Romantic. A view of life that has no base in fact, being the product of an exaggerated optimism.

Semantics. (1) Science of the study of the development of the meaning and uses of words and language; (2) the exploitation of the connotations and ambiguities in words.

Substantial. A term used to denote the extent of healing in the relationships of man with God, with his fellow man and within himself which should be seen in the life of a Christian—not perfect and yet visible in reality.

Surrealism. An art form which produces fantastic or incongruous imagery by means of unnatural juxtapositions and combinations, related to Dada plus the subconscious.

Synthesis. The combination of the partial truths of a thesis and its antithesis into a higher stage of truth; cf. Dialectic.

"Upper Story." Term used to denote that which, in modern thinking, deals with significance or meaning, but which is not open to contact with verification by the world of facts which constitute the "lower story."

Validity. Something which has been authenticated by reference to well-grounded and sufficient evidence.

Verbalization. The putting of a proposition into words.

Verification. The procedure required for the establishment of the truth or falsity of a statement.

Notes

Introduction
[1]*Escape from Reason* (1968) was the first of the two books to be published in England by IVP-UK in the spring of 1968, but it derived from lectures given after those at Wheaton College in 1965 that became *The God Who Is There* (1968).

[2]Richard Rorty, *Contingency, Irony and Solidarity* (Cambridge: Cambridge University Press, 1989), p. 7.

Section I
Chapter 1: The Gulf Is Fixed
[1]The consideration of classical and presuppositional apologetics is continued in section III, chapter 5, p. 137. Also see appendix A.

[2]Julian Huxley, ed., *The Humanist Frame* (London: Allen and Unwin, 1961).

[3]James 1:27.

Chapter 2: The First Step in the Line of Despair: Philosophy
[1]Cf., e.g., Professor A. J. Ayer in *What I Believe*, ed. Unwin (London: Allen and Unwin, 1966); and Antony Flew, "Must Morality Pay?" *Listener*, October 13, 1966.

[2]Julian Huxley, ed., *The Humanist Frame* (London: Allen and Unwin, 1961), p. 46.

[3]Ibid., p. 409.

[4]*Tibetan Book of the Dead* (New York: University Books, 1964).

Chapter 3: The Second Step: Art
[1]See pp. 81-82.

[2]This is the translation suggested by Dr. H. R. Rookmaaker in *Synthetist Art Theories* (Amsterdam, 1959); p. 23, and note w to chapter 9.

[3]A letter written in February 1898.

[4]Rookmaaker, *Synthetist Art Theories*, notes n, p, aa, af to chapter 9.

[5]Two works with Eva's name written on them were exhibited in the Picasso and Man Exhibition at the Toronto Art Gallery, January 1964.

[6]Hans Arp, "Für Theo van Doesburg," *De Stijl*, January 1932.

Chapter 4: The Third & Fourth Steps: Music & the General Culture
[1]See paragraph on the Beatles, p. 62.

[2]Ducretet-Thomson, Paris, no. 320 c. 100.

[3]Dylan Thomas, "Elegy," *Collected Poems, 1934-52* (London: J. M. Dent and Sons, 1959), pp. 179-80.

[4]*Revolver*, The Beatles, S.M.O. Records, 81.045, 1967.

[5]John Lennon and Paul McCartney, "Strawberry Fields Forever" and "Penny Lane," in *Magical Mystery Tour*, The Beatles, EMI Records, R5570, 1967.

[6]*Sgt. Pepper's Lonely Hearts Club Band*, The Beatles, EMI Records, PMC 7027, 1967.

Chapter 5: The Unifying Factor in the Steps of Despair
[1]Léopold Sédar Senghor, *On African Socialism* (New York: Frederick A. Praeger, 1964).

[2]Léopold Sédar Senghor, *Selected Poems* (Oxford University Press, 1964).

[3]French Jesuit paleontologist who wrote *The Phenomenon of Man* (London: Collins; New York: Harper & Row, 1959), and other books.

[4]Sir Julian Huxley wrote the introduction to the British edition of *The Phenomenon of Man* in 1958. In this he agrees both with the methodology and broad conclusions of Teilhard de Chardin regarding the evolutionary future of man. Later, in 1961, he develops his general agreement with these conclusions in the direction of the use of religion in his introduction to *The Humanist Frame*. What Senghor does in his book in applying Teilhard de Chardin's principles to the state of Senegal, Huxley seeks to do on a global scale.
[5]Cf. 1 Corinthians 15:13-14, 32.

Section II
Chapter 1: The Fifth Step: Theology
[1]In regard to Kierkegaard, it is important to keep in mind what is stated on pp. 34-36.

Chapter 2: Modern Mysticism: Despair Beyond Despair
[1]My thinking has led me to believe that there is a collective cultural consciousness or memory which is related to words. I would suggest there are two parts to it: a collective memory of a specific race, and a collective memory of all men as to what man is and what reality is.

Thus man, in his *language*, "remembers" (regardless of his personal belief) that God does exist. For example, when the Russian leaders curse, they curse by God, and not by something less; and atheistic artists often use "god" symbols. This, I believe, is a deeper yet simpler explanation than Jung's view of god as the supreme archetype arising (according to him) out of the evolution of the race. Moreover, in man's language, man also remembers that humanity is unique (created in the image of God), and therefore words like *purpose, love, morals* carry with them in connotation their real meaning. This is the case regardless of the individual's personal worldview and despite what the dictionary or scientific textbook definition has become.

At times the connotation of the word is deeper and more "unconscious" than its definition. The use of such words trigger responses to a greater degree in line with what the specific race has thought they mean and how it has acted on their meaning, and to a lesser degree in line with what really is and what man is. I would further suggest that after the worldview and experiences of the race form the definition and connotation of the words of any specific language, then that language as a symbol system becomes the vehicle for keeping alive and teaching this worldview and experience.

It would therefore seem to me that the whole matter is primarily one of language, as man thinks and communicates in language. I would say that in this context the division of languages at the tower of Babel is an overwhelmingly profound moment of history.
[2]Giovanni Gentile, *Leonardo da Vinci* (New York: Raynal, 1956), p. 174.
[3]I am consciously omitting here the intermediate and important change in the formulation at the time of Kant (1724-1804) and Rousseau (1712-1778). That formulation was:

Freedom

Nature

See Francis A. Schaeffer, *Escape From Reason* (Downers Grove, Ill.: InterVarsity Press, 1968), pp. 32-36; and in *The Complete Works of Francis A. Schaeffer* (Wheaton, Ill.: Crossway Books, 1982), 1:227-29.

Chapter 3: Modern Mysticism in Action: Art & Language
[1]Sylvia Sprigge, *Berenson: A Biography* (Boston: Houghton Mifflin, 1960).
[2]Cf. 1 Corinthians 15:6.
[3]Published in 1920.
[4]In the same way, you have a parallel situation with the two women Picasso married. One is a very human picture of Olga, painted in 1917-1918, the other is a lovely painting of Jacqueline done on October 5, 1954. There is a further parallel in that Jacqueline keeps this drawing in

her sitting room. In these paintings it is not only that the painting speaks of the love of the artist for his wife, but the woman has meaning as a human being.

[5]Since his painting of the *Basket of Bread*, he has painted many pictures in which a Mary-like figure is the focus-point of the painting. The Gallery of Modern Art in New York has some of these paintings in which the figure appears several times in one painting. However, on inspection, one sees that these Mary-like figures are portraits of Dali's wife.

[6]Martin Heidegger, *What Is Philosophy?* (London: Vision Press, 1956).

Chapter 4: Modern Mysticism in Action: Music & Literature

[1]Leonard Bernstein, Third Symphony, New York Philharmonic, Columbia KL 6005 or KS 6005.

[2]Calvin Tomkins, "Profile of John Cage," *New Yorker*, November 28, 1964.

[3]Because his theories have produced in music noise or total silence, which is therefore monotonous, most modern music has not followed him. But through Merce Cunningham and others, John Cage has become the central force in some modern dance, against Martha Graham who put much emphasis on form and meaning.

[4]The translation of this preface is that which appeared in *Vogue*, December 1964.

Chapter 5: The Next Phase of Modern Theology

[1]In recent years it has often been said that Karl Barth changed his views toward the end of his life. If this was so, then all could have been easily cared for by his writing one more book amongst his many books and, while he was yet living, making it known that his views of Scripture, his lack of a space-time Fall, and his implicit universalism had been publicly repudiated. In the light of his crucial influence as the originator of the new theology and his wide publication, it would seem difficult to think that anything less would have met his responsibility before God and men. If he had done this, many of us would have truly rejoiced. Note pp. 130-31 for a consideration of the deficient concept of justification and the place of universalism in the new theology.

[2]The italics are mine.

[3]As an example, see Dr. Alan Richardson, "When Is a Word an Event?" *Listener*, June 3, 1965.

[4]Raymond Panikkar, *The Unknown Christ of Hinduism* (London: Darton, Longman and Todd, 1964).

[5]Dom Bede Griffiths, *Jubilee*, November 1963.

[6]Anthony de Mello at a Loyola University ecumenical forum as reported in the Chicago *Daily News-Post Dispatch*, December 14, 1963.

Section III

Chapter 1: Personality or a Devilish Din

[1]In John 17:24 Jesus, in his prayer to his Father, speaks of the love with which "thou lovedst me before the foundation of the world." In Genesis 1:26 there is reported communication within the Trinity.

[2]Henrik Ibsen, *The Wild Duck*.

Chapter 2: Verifiable Facts & Knowing

[1]J. S. Bezzant, *Objections to Christian Belief* (London: Constable), pp. 90, 91.

[2]Exodus 24:12.

[3]Acts 26:14.

[4]John 17:24.

Chapter 3: The Dilemma of Man

[1]Albert Camus, *The Plague*, trans. Stuart Gilbert (London: Hamish Hamilton; Penguin Books,

1966 [*La Peste,* 1947]).

[2]The consideration of *The Plague* is continued on pp. 135-36.

[3]John 5:24; Colossians 1:13.

[4]Genesis 2:17.

[5]It is intriguing that the "new" Heidegger, as he changed his position, tried to get a historic Fall into his new system. He says there was a Golden Age (before this Fall) at the time of the pre-Socratic Greeks; and then Aristotle, and those who followed him, fell. He says that their fall was that they began to think rationally. So Heidegger is saying that man is abnormal. There is no historic evidence for such a Golden Age, and certainly it is not correct that before Aristotle people did not think rationally, but it does indicate that the usual rationalistic answer to man's dilemma, which says man is as he has always been, is insufficient. In Heidegger's desperate theory, Aristotle takes the place of Adam, as the one who fell, and it does appear as if Heidegger sees himself as the one who will save. But notice that this concept of the Fall and salvation does not touch moral issues. Man's abnormality is not moral; in Heidegger's new system it is rather epistemological and methodological abnormality. Aristotle was not morally wrong in what he did, according to Heidegger; he was just introducing the faulty methodology of antithesis and rationality. There is no answer here for man's dilemma, but Heidegger has clearly shown that philosophy has no answer to man's dilemma on the basis of man and history now being normal. It would seem that Heidegger would like Christianity's answer, but without bowing to God— either morally or in acknowledging the need of knowledge from him.

Chapter 4: God's Answer to Man's Dilemma

[1]Cf. p. 130.

[2]Simone de Beauvoir deals with the same problem in a slightly different setting in her book *A Very Easy Death* (New York: Putnam, 1966).

[3]See B. B. Warfield, "On the Emotional Life of Our Lord," in *Biblical and Theological Studies* (New York: Scribner's, 1912), pp. 35-90.

Chapter 5: How Do We Know It Is True?

[1]"As the archrevolutionary Einstein says: 'The historical development has shown that among the imaginable theoretical constructions there is invariably one that proves to be unquestionably superior to all others. Nobody who really goes into the matter will deny that the world of perceptions determines the theoretical system in a virtually unambiguous manner.' A man engaged in solving a well designed word-puzzle may, it is true, propose any word as the solution, but there is only *one* word which really solves the puzzle in all its forms. It is an outcome of faith that nature takes the character of such a well-formulated puzzle. The successes reaped up to now by science do, it is true, give a certain encouragement for this faith." (H. R. Post, "Scientific Theories," *Listener,* February 10, 1966)

[2]Romans 1:18-20 RV.

[3]In an article in the *Christian Century* of May 12, 1965, entitled "The Modernity of Fundamentalism," John Opie Jr. makes two main mistakes. He says correctly that historic Christianity (which he calls fundamentalism) is primarily separated from the new theology not in theological detail but in epistemology and methodology, because it insists on rationality. However, he then goes on to say that historic Christianity is interested *exclusively* in rationality. This is not so. The other mistake he makes, a foolish one, is his saying that the kind of thinking upon which Christianity is based—that is, rational thinking—began with the Enlightenment. This view has no more support that Heidegger's when he says that it began with Aristotle, and is even more impossible to support. Other men in the new theology have made this same mistake. For example, Ernest R. Sandeen in his article "The Princeton Theology," *Church History,* September 1962.

[4]See appendix A under rationalism.
[5]1 John 4:1-3.

Section IV
Chapter 1: Finding the Point of Tension
[1]Acts 17:26.
[2]Psalm 139:8.
[3]Romans 1:32—2:3.

Chapter 2: From the Point of Tension to the Gospel
[1]See section I, p. 27.
[2]The basic concepts presented here were put forth first in my article entitled "A Review of a Review," *Bible Today* 42, no. 1 (October 1948).

Romans 1:18 reads, "For the wrath of God is revealed from heaven against all ungodliness and unrighteousness of men, who hold the truth in unrighteousness." The context shows that this "holding the truth in unrighteousness" is related to the "general revelation" of the "mannishness" of man and the external universe in verses 19 and 20. The concept involved in the phrase "who hold the truth in unrighteousness" has two possibilities: in many of the newer translations it is translated as *hinder, hold down, stifle, restrain* or *suppress* the truth—which men have from the general revelation of the external creation and man's "mannishness." Probably a more accurate meaning, from the Greek word used, is that they *hold* that portion of the truth of the real world that they must hold (in spite of their non-Christian presuppositions); but because of their unrighteousness, their rebellion, they do not carry the logic of the general revelation to its natural and proper conclusion. Thus they are in the strict sense without excuse.

Chapter 3: Applying the Gospel
[1]Hebrews 11:6.
[2]Acts 16:30-32.
[3]Bunyan's note at this place is "Come unto me, all ye that labour and are heavy laden, and I will give you rest" (Matthew 11:28).
[4]The ninth stage of *Pilgrim's Progress*.
[5]The following references in the Bible will help anyone who wants to read more about becoming a Christian: John 3:15-18; Romans 3:9-26; 4:1-3; Galatians 2:16; 3:24; John 8:24; 14:6; Acts 4:12. Romans chapters 1—8 is a good section in which to see the unity of becoming a Christian and what follows after one is a Christian.

Section V
Chapter 1: Commending the Christian Faith to Our Generation
[1]John 20:30, 31.
[2]Luke 1:1-4.

Chapter 2: The Importance of Truth
[1]Mark 12:30; Deuteronomy 6:5.

Section VI
Chapter 1: Demonstrating the Character of God
[1]John 13:34, 35; 17:21.
[2]Matthew 5:48.
[3]1 John 2:1.

[4]Romans 7:22-25.
[5]2 Corinthians 13:14.

Appendix A: The Question of Apologetics

[1]Concerning the Philippian jailer, see pp. 163-65.

[2]*He Is There and He Is Not Silent* (Wheaton, Ill.: Tyndale House, 1972), also found in *The Complete Works of Francis A. Schaeffer*, vol. 1 (Wheaton, Ill.: Crossway Books, 1982), deals with the metaphysical, the moral and the epistemological necessity.

Index